CAV HAT

U.S. Army Cavalry Hat

The Proud Legacy
and Enduring
Traditions

Rex Gooch

**Lighthorse Publishing
Company**
Sioux Falls, SD 57104

Copyright © 2025 by Rex Gooch

All rights reserved. No part of this publication may be reproduced or transmitted in any form or by any means electronic or mechanical, including photocopy, recording, or any information storage and retrieval system now known or to be invented, without permission in writing from the author, except by a reviewer who wishes to quote brief passages in connection with a review written for inclusion in a magazine, newspaper, website article, or broadcast.

ISBN: 979-8-9916287-4-7
Library of Congress Control Number: 2025919794

Front cover photo: Bob Monette's Cav Hat
Rear cover photo: George Abernathy's Cav Hat

This book is dedicated to
every Cavalry trooper
who proudly wore
or is presently wearing
a Cav Hat.

Table of Contents

Foreword i
About the Author iii
Preface v

PART 1   THE CAMPAIGN HAT 1
  Chapter 1   Civil War Era 3
    THE BIRTH OF THE U.S CAVALRY – 1855 3
    U.S. CAVALRY HARDEE HATS 4
    U.S. ARMY HAT 5
    THE 1858 FORAGE CAP 7
    CIVIL WAR SLOUCH HAT 9
  Chapter 2   Indian Wars 11
    POST-CIVIL WAR 11
    CAMPAIGN HATS 13
    1876 CAMPAIGN HAT 15
    "DRAB" COLOR 18
    1883 CAMPAIGN HAT 19
    INDIAN WARS 20
    BUFFALO SOLDIER CAVALRY 22
    TEDDY ROOSEVELT AND THE ROUGH RIDERS 25
    CAVALRY MOVIES 28

PART 2   THE CAVALRY HAT 31
  Chapter 3   Birth of the Cav Hat 33
    TESTING THE AIR CAVALRY CONCEPT 33
    ORIGINATION OF THE CAVALRY HAT 34

  CAVALRY HAT BACKSTORY...... 35
  LTC STOCKTON'S BIRTHDAY PRESENT 37
  NEW SOURCE FOR CAVALRY HATS 39
  YOU CAN'T WEAR THAT HERE 39
  CAVALRY STETSONS IN VIETNAM 41
  CAVALRY PRIDE...... 44

Chapter 4 Vietnam Cav Hat Stories......45
  "MY CAV HAT TOOK HITS"...... 45
  "I WANNA BE A SCOUT PILOT"...... 51
  A PURPLE HEART FOR MY CAV HAT...... 55
  "MY CAV HAT WAS KIDNAPPED BY THE MARINES"...... 59
  B TROOP GUNS 65
  "MY CAV HAT DECIDED TO FLY"...... 69
  "YOU SHOT MY CAV HAT!"...... 73
  THE "QUAKER HAT"...... 81
  "I EXTENDED MY TOUR FOR A CAV HAT"...... 83
  "DID YOU GET MY CAV HAT?"...... 87
  THE HIPPIE HAT BAND AND THE PEACOCK 95
  "THE VC SHOT MY CAV HAT AND HIT MY COFFEE"...... 97
  SILVERBELLY CAV HATS – LIGHTHORSE AIR CAVALRY...... 103
  "BILLY JACK" CAV HATS 107
  "DID I JUST GIVE MY CAV HAT TO A NAVY NURSE?"...... 109
  "HELL NO, I'M NOT REMOVING MY CAV HAT!" 113
  MY "GABBY HAYES" CAV HAT 119
  "WHERE'S YOUR CAV HAT?"...... 123
  THE SMILING TIGER SCOUTS HAT BAND 125
  FATHER AND SON CAV HAT...... 127
  THE CAV GUY 131
  THE OUTCASTS 135
  NOW AND THEN 137
  "THE COWBOYS STOLE MY CAV HAT"...... 139
  CHARLIE HORSE GUNS 141

Chapter 5 Cav Hats in Iraq 145
Chapter 6 Cav Hats in Afghanistan 153
  SILVERBELLY CAV HATS RETURN – CRAZYHORSE......156
Chapter 7 Cav Hats in Europe......165

GERMANY CAV HATS 165
POLAND CAV HATS 171
SLOVAKIA CAV HATS 176
CROATIA CAV HATS 177
HUNGARY CAV HATS 178
FINLAND CAV HATS 179

Chapter 8   Squadron and Regiment Cav Hats 181
3RD CAVALRY REGIMENT – BRAVE RIFLES 183
11TH ARMORED CAVALRY REGIMENT – BLACKHORSE 191
1ST SQUADRON, 17TH CAVALRY REGIMENT 197
2ND SQUADRON, 17TH CAVALRY REGIMENT 201
3RD SQUADRON, 17TH CAVALRY REGIMENT 205
5TH SQUADRON, 17TH CAVALRY REGIMENT 211
7TH SQUADRON, 17TH CAVALRY REGIMENT 215
1ST SQUADRON, 6TH CAVALRY REGIMENT 221
2ND SQUADRON, 6TH CAVALRY REGIMENT 225
4TH SQUADRON, 6TH CAVALRY REGIMENT 231
6TH SQUADRON, 6TH CAVALRY REGIMENT 237

Chapter 9   Horse Cavalry Detachment 241
1ST CAVALRY DIVISION HORSE DETACHMENT 243

Chapter 10   Cav Hat Creases and Brims 251

Chapter 11   Cav Hat Traditions 259
"BREAKING-IN" CEREMONY 259
FIDDLER'S GREEN 265
COMBAT KNOTS 266

Chapter 12   Army Humor 267
STETSON – "THE OFFICIAL ARMY HEADGEAR" 267

Chapter 13   Cav Hat Standards 271

Chapter 14   Cav Hat Finale 277

APPENDIX I 279
VIETNAM CAV HAT STORIES TERMINOLOGY 279

APPENDIX II 283
SOUTH VIETNAM MAP 283

INDEX 285

The Cav Hat in Vietnam
First Lieutenant Larry Brown
C Troop, 3rd of the 17th Air Cavalry
Quang Tri, South Vietnam, August 1970
Photo Courtesy of Larry Brown

Photo on Previous Page

This iconic photo of First Lieutenant Larry Brown wearing his Cav Hat was taken at Quang Tri in August 1970 while he was flying scouts for "Charlie Horse," C Troop, 3rd Squadron, 17th Air Cavalry. Larry's cavalry hat is adorned with brass from the 1st of the 9th Cavalry, a tribute to his first Vietnam tour.

The Charlie Horse scouts played a vital role in a test program that assessed the combat effectiveness of the OH-58 Kiowa scout helicopter. Brown was chosen for this program because of his experience flying scouts during his first tour and his background as a flight instructor. The insights provided by the Charlie Horse scouts were essential in validating the Kiowa's capabilities and ensuring its combat readiness.

The photo was taken by a photographer from the Red Devil newspaper, the publication of the 5th Mechanized Infantry Division. In the image, Larry is sitting in the door of his OH-58 scout helicopter.

In December 1970, Larry transferred to Echo Troop, 1st of the 9th Air Cavalry based out of Lai Khe in III Corps. Brown was the scout platoon leader flying the OH-6A helicopter. You can read Larry's story, titled "You Shot My Cav Hat!," in Chapter 4 of this book.

Foreword

The Cavalry Hat, often referred to as the "Cav Hat," stands as one of the most iconic and distinctive elements of the U.S. Army uniform. Rooted in the proud tradition of the Army's legendary horse cavalry, this remarkable hat embodies a powerful legacy, and its unique design inspires wearers to honor the courageous spirit of those who have served before them.

I was incredibly fortunate that my first unit was the 2nd Squadron (RECON), 9th Cavalry, in the 7th Infantry Division (LIGHT). This distinguished cavalry squadron was led by many combat-seasoned veterans of the Vietnam War. It was here that I earned my spurs, donned the revered Cav Hat, and first faced the reality of combat.

Serving alongside soldiers who had exemplified the spirit of cavalry troopers in Vietnam, I was profoundly inspired by their unwavering professionalism and fighting spirit. Their deep commitment to sharing their combat experiences empowered me and shaped my understanding of the responsibility we have to train and mentor the next generation of warriors.

Throughout my thirty-eight years in the Army, the 2nd of the 9th Cavalry has stood out as one of my favorite units. It served as a remarkable breeding ground for exceptional leaders, with two of our own rising to the ranks of the Joint Chiefs of Staff. Even today, many of us maintain strong connections, often reminiscing about our shared adventures while proudly wearing or drinking from our Cav Hats. These hats not only symbolize our commitment to one another but also embody the enduring camaraderie that continues to thrive among us, undiminished by the passage of time.

Any soldier who has earned the right to wear a Cav Hat understands its significance and the esprit de corps it represents. Cavalry units not only work hard but also celebrate their achievements with unmatched enthusiasm. The Cav Hat has always been at the heart of that hard work and celebration, symbolizing the remarkable experiences and shared triumphs that define the cavalry journey.

In *Cav Hat*, Rex Gooch compiles not only the history of the cavalry hat but, more importantly, the stories behind those who wore it while serving our country in war. We should all be grateful for the time and research Rex dedicated to telling the story of the Cav Hat and honoring those who have earned the right to wear it.

General (Ret) Daniel R. Hokanson
29th Chief of the National Guard Bureau

About the Author

Rex Gooch is a U.S. Army combat veteran who served in the Vietnam War flying Huey helicopters for C Troop, 3rd of the 17th Air Cavalry, proudly known as Lighthorse. Through this profound experience, he forged a strong bond and "Cavalry Pride" with his air cavalry brothers. This pride is embodied by the Cav Hat, a powerful symbol of the troopers' unwavering commitment to the U.S. Cavalry and its rich heritage.

Rex has written and published two award-winning books about Army Aviation during the Vietnam War. His first book, *ACE: The Story of Lt. Col. Ace Cozzalio*, tells the incredible story of war hero Ace Cozzalio, highlighting his exploits and adventures while flying helicopters for Lighthorse Air Cavalry in Vietnam. This book was awarded the Bronze Medal in the nonfiction category of the 2016 Independent Publishers Book Awards.

Rex's second book, *The Aviators: Stories of U.S. Army Helicopter Combat in the Vietnam War, 1971-72,* narrates the stories of young aviators, fresh out of flight school, who gallantly serve their country in a controversial war in a foreign land. This book won the Bronze Medal in the Best eBook category at the 2020 Independent Publishers Book Awards.

Rex Gooch

Preface

The cavalry hat has a rich and storied history that dates back to the formation of the U.S. Cavalry in 1855. Since then, cavalry soldiers and troopers have proudly worn their distinctive headgear, complete with hat decorations and insignia that distinguish them from other Army units.

This book is a long-overdue tribute to the iconic cavalry hat. Part 1 of this book explores the history of this proud tradition, tracing the evolution of the cavalry's first hat, the Hardee Hat, to the post-Civil War Campaign Hat. Part 2 delves into the emergence of the Cav Hat in the early days of the Vietnam War and shares unique, engaging, and often unusual stories about modern cavalry troopers and their cavalry hats. Subsequent chapters tell of Cav Hats worn in Iraq, Afghanistan, Europe, and the squadrons and regiments of today's cavalry. To conclude, the later chapters discuss Cav Hat traditions, creases, and standards.

I hope you enjoy reading about the revered Cav Hat and its proud and storied heritage.

Rex Gooch
Longknife 23
C Troop, 3rd of the 17th Air Cavalry

Rex Gooch

PART 1
THE CAMPAIGN HAT

Rex Gooch

CHAPTER 1

CIVIL WAR ERA

THE BIRTH OF THE U.S CAVALRY – 1855

The resolution of the Oregon boundary dispute in 1846 and the victory over Mexico in 1848 significantly expanded the territory of the Union and vastly increased the responsibilities of the Army. However, following the conclusion of the War with Mexico, the Army was reduced to a peacetime strength smaller than that authorized after the War of 1812. As a result, the Army struggled to oversee this vast expanse of frontier land.

It was only after Jefferson Davis, a West Point graduate and a volunteer regimental commander in the Mexican-American War, became secretary of war in 1853 that some relief was finally obtained. At the urging of Davis, Congress authorized the formation of the 1st and 2nd Cavalry Regiments for frontier service on March 3, 1855. This marked the creation of the U.S. Cavalry, a unit that distinguished itself by fighting on horseback with sabers and firearms, rather than the dragoons who fought either mounted or on foot.

General Order No. 4, dated March 26, 1855, mandated that cavalry units be uniformed in a manner similar to their older counterparts, the dragoons. However, the trimmings on the cavalry's hat and coat were to be yellow instead of the traditional orange. As a result, the cavalry branch color, which has remained unchanged to this day, was established.

U.S. CAVALRY HARDEE HATS

In July 1855, a board of newly appointed cavalry regiment officers convened to decide on the cavalry's arms, uniforms, and horse equipment. In their report, the board specified a hat to be worn exclusively by the cavalry. This cavalry hat became known by several nicknames, the most widely recognized being the "Hardee" hat.

1855 Enlisted Cavalry Hat
Courtesy Heritage
Auctions/HA.com

1LT Giles F. Ward Jr.
Company L, 12th New York Cavalry
Courtesy Library of Congress

Crafted from black felt, this hat featured a folded brim on one side with a large eagle insignia attaching the brim to the side of the crown. Additionally, the hat was equipped with a chin strap. Field officers' hats were adorned with a gold cord wrapped around the base of the crown, and three black feathers adorned the side opposite the folded brim. The regiment number was displayed on the crown front. Enlisted men wore the same hat but with a worsted cord instead of a gold cord and one black feather opposite the folded side. The company letter replaced the regiment number on the crown front.

U.S. ARMY HAT

It wasn't long before the commanders of artillery, dragoons, and other units requested the issuance of Hardee hats for their respective units. In response to these requests, a special board of army officers convened to recommend a new hat for the entire army. In February 1858, the board included the following statement in their recommendations to the secretary of war: "The hat proposed (Hardee) is in the opinion of the Board equally suitable for troops of all arms of the service and it is accordingly recommended for the whole Army..."

The specifications for the new army hat were generally identical to the cavalry hat with the following stipulations. The hat was to be crafted from the finest black felt with a brim width of three and one-fourth inches and a crown height of six and one-fourth inches. The hat trimmings were described as follows:

General Officers

> The hat was adorned with gold cord wrapped around the base of the crown with acorn-shaped ends. A large eagle emblem held the brim folded to the side of the crown, and three black ostrich feathers were attached to the non-folded side. The front of the crown was adorned with a gold-embroidered wreath encircling old English characters "US" in silver sewn on a black velvet background.

Field Officers (above the rank of captain)

The hat was the same as general officers' except the hat cord was black silk and gold.

Officers

Same as field officers except the hat displayed two ostrich feathers.

Enlisted men

The hat cords were worsted and adorned with one feather. As with the calvary, the hat displayed the company letter on the front of the crown.

1858 Infantry Enlisted Hat
Courtesy The Horse Soldier

Union Sergeants – Company B,
3rd California Infantry – 1858 Army Hat
Photo Courtesy of Ronald S. Coddington

Initially, there was confusion regarding which side of the hat featured the folded brim. Later, in 1861, General Order 6 stated "that the brim was to be looped up on the right by mounted men and on the left by foot soldiers."

Thus, the Hardee hat, originally worn by the cavalry, was adopted by all branches of the service during the Civil War. The hats were stylish for the day and had a striking appearance on the parade ground or around the garrison, but soldiers soon found them heavy, hot, and impractical in the field.

The 1858 Forage Cap

Although not traditionally considered a "Campaign or Cavalry hat," the forage cap in the "French kepi style" was worn by both cavalry officers and enlisted men during the Civil War, making it worthy of attention in this book.

During the 1850s, the Army recognized a need for a hat specifically designed for "fatigue duty" and field use. This was particularly evident with the engineering troops, who were essentially skilled laborers. Their commanders repeatedly requested a fatigue hat for field use.

In 1856, Captain George B. McClellan, on his return from an inspection tour of the European armies, recommended "a visorless forage cap that could be folded and carried in pack or saddle bag, he did speak in some detail of the French forage cap, describing it as having a large straight visor and a loose conical top."

The call for a "fatigue duty" hat was further reinforced by a letter to the adjutant general from Brevet Major William H. French, Commanding Officer at Fort McHenry, Maryland, requesting permission for his men to wear fatigue caps, and he submitted four prototype caps for consideration.

French's request was forwarded to the secretary of war, who issued General Order No. 13, stating:

> For fatigue purposes Forage Caps, of pattern in the Quartermaster General's Office, will be issued, in addition to hats, at the rate of one a year. Dark blue cloth, with a cord or welt around the crown of the colors used to distinguish the several arms of service, and yellow metal letters in front to designate companies. For unassigned recruits dark blue cord or welt around the crown and without distinctive badge. Commissioned officers may wear

caps of the same pattern with dark blue welt and the distinctive ornament, in front, of the corps and regiment.

Cavalry Enlisted Forage Cap
Courtesy Morphy Auctions

Captain Comly J. Mather
Co B&F, 15th Pennsylvania Cavalry
McClellan Version of Forage Hat
Courtesy Library of Congress

Comments on the cap varied from good to bad, but overall, they were viewed as an improvement over previous hats. One complained that it was a "waste of cloth, too baggy, and caught the wind," while another called it "useful and even natty," though not particularly beautiful. Another said, "No other cap is so comfortable."

The forage cap was quite popular during the Civil War and became even more favored when officers started wearing the non-regulation "McClellan style" hat. This hat resembled the forage cap, but its main difference was the shorter dimensions at the front and rear of the crown, giving it a sleek, less floppy appearance.

Civil War Slouch Hat

During the Civil War years, officers wore a wide variety of hats, with non-regulation styles outnumbering the regulation ones by a wide margin. It was during this time that the slouch hat gained immense popularity and eventually became the preferred headgear of many Union officers.

The name "slouch hat" refers to the fact that one brim droops down, as opposed to the other, which is pinned against the side of the crown. The style was highly variable and personal, with various types of crowns, crown heights, and brim widths.[1] For practical purposes, many chose to wear the brim down on all sides.

The most recognized version of the slouch hat was made from soft black felt. It featured a crown height of five to seven inches, and its brim measured three to three and a half inches wide. This design provided excellent protection from both the sun and rain, making it ideal for soldiers enduring the harshest weather conditions. Soldiers shaped the brims of their hats to meet practical needs and often decorated them with personal touches, such as feathers or badges, to express their individuality and pride.

One distinctive feature of the slouch hat was a half-inch grosgrain ribbon sewn around the edge of the brim. The advent of sewing machines in the mid-1800s revolutionized hat-making, making this stylish detail popular and a mark of quality craftsmanship.

During the Civil War, the production and distribution of uniforms presented a significant challenge. The slouch hat emerged as a practical solution, as it was quicker to manufacture,

---

[1] Klein, Lloyd W. "U.S. Civil War Hats . *History Is Now* agazine. December 23, 2024. https://www.historyisnowmagazine.com/blog/2024/12/23/us-civil-war-hats.

enabling local hatters to meet the pressing demand more efficiently. While not a regulation hat, it is reported that Union quartermasters adopted the slouch hat for issue in 1864.[2]

Slouch Hat Worn by
General John Henry Hobard Ward
Courtesy Heritage Auctions/HA.com

2LT Emil Beese, Co C, 12th NY Cavalry
1865 Slouch Hat
Courtesy Library of Congress

---

[2] "Civil War Cowboy Hats in History - Slouch Hats," https://www.cowboyhathistory.org/civil_war/civil_war.html.

CHAPTER 2
INDIAN WARS

POST-CIVIL WAR

After the Civil War, the U.S. Army fell upon hard times. By September 1866, the size of the Regular Establishment, which included the Army, was drastically reduced from hundreds of thousands of personnel to just 39,000. As a result, the Army was left with a huge surplus of uniforms, arms, and equipment that could only be sold on the open market at a significant loss. This situation would have prompted screams of anguish from a fiscally conscious Congress, so the items had to be used. It was during these times that the Army's role was redefined, creating a compelling need for an updated uniform that reflected its evolving mission.

Thomas Nast (1840-1902) was a renowned caricaturist and political cartoonist who contributed drawings to *Harper's Weekly* from 1859 to 1860 and again from 1862 to 1886. Through these cartoons, Nast, a Republican and supporter of the military, ridiculed and condemned the Democratic Congress for even the suggestion of reducing the U.S. Army during an era of Indian warfare on the frontier. More specifically, these cartoons lampooned the House of Representatives bill, H. R. 2546, which provided for the gradual reduction of the Army of the United States.³

Harper's Weekley Cartoon – July 27, 1874
"Our Living Skeleton Standing Army" by Thomas Nast

In 1868, in response to the Army's changing role and needs, Assistant Surgeon General Alfred A. Woodhull researched and submitted "A Medical Report upon the Uniform and Clothing of the Soldiers of the U.S. Army," more commonly called the "Woodhull Report," which represented the consensus of more than 120 professional soldiers and Army surgeons. The

---

³ "Those Who Served: The U. S. Army on the Frontier - National Cowboy &Amp; Western Heritage Museum." 2019. National Cowboy & Western Heritage Museum. May 9, 2019. https://nationalcowboymuseum.org/explore/served-u-s-army-frontier/.

purpose of this report was to identify health-related issues with Army uniforms, especially the headgear, and to suggest improvements for future designs.

In Woodall's report, he stated that the Hardee-style hat was too heavy and its visor obstructed vision, and it offered no protection from the sun or rain. Moreover, its color amplified the transmission of solar heat. In Woodall's conclusions, he recommended, "A light-colored, brimmed felt hat… The brim should have a width about equal to the height of the crown."

Despite its supposed practicality and the pressure exerted on the War Department to adopt it, the 1858 Hardee hat received overwhelmingly negative feedback. Civil War photographs reveal that the forage or "kepi cap" worn mostly by enlisted men far outnumbered the 1858 hat by a significant margin, exceeding one hundred to one.

Comments from those wearing the Hardee hat ran from "nuisance" and "heavy, hot, stiff, and ill-looking" to "abomination" and "unsightly abortion." One correspondent wrote to the *Army and Navy Journal*: "Many regiments refused to draw them, while others promptly discarded them after drawing them." Another wrote: "The black felt hat is so much disliked by the entire Army, that it is never worn for even dress occasions if it can be avoided and in a garrison you cannot see two officers equipped alike." Several others suggested replacing it with a lightweight gray or dust-colored felt hat.

Campaign Hats

By 1871, the excess supply of uniforms was depleted, and the usable uniform supply was running low. There were ongoing requests for both replenishment and a change in Army uniforms. In July 1871, the secretary of war instructed the general in chief to form a board of officers. This board was tasked with developing "General Regulations," which included, among other aspects, modifications to the Army uniform. The board's recommendations, issued in War Department General Orders Nos. 76 and 92, issued 29 July and 26 October 1872, respectively, prescribed an almost entirely new uniform for the officers and enlisted men of the Army.

For headgear, the board adopted a hat of black animal fur felt "to be worn only on fatigue duty and on marches and campaigns." Although the term "fatigue hat" was used in the regulations, it quickly dropped out of favor and was replaced with the term "campaign." This new hat had a wide, elliptical-shaped, flat brim measuring five inches on each side and four and one-half inches on the front and rear. Its crown stood five and a half inches top to bottom without the crease. At the base of the crown was a one-inch-wide ribbed silk ribbon with a bow on one side.

This uniquely shaped hat, with its elliptical brim, was designed to fold flat for easy storage when not in use. By turning the side brims upward toward the crown and securing them with two sets of hooks and eyes attached to the brim's outer edge, the hat maintained a flattened triangular shape. The officer's hats differed from the enlisted models only in quality and the addition of a black silk binding on the edge of the brim.

Reaction to the new hat was somewhat slow, but comments soon ranged from "worthless" to "complete failure." The criticism was echoed at the highest level by Brevet Major General Edmund Schriver, inspector general of the Army, who stated, "Ridiculous in design [and] faulty in manufacture…better suited to a wet nurse than a soldier in the ranks…I state this without fear of contradiction."

1872 Campaign Hat
Courtesy of Centurion Auctions

CPT George Armstrong
Co D, 7th Michigan Cavalry
Courtesy Library of Congress

The outspoken criticism of the 1872 hat primarily focused on its lack of durability. However, much of the correspondence also included criticism of the black color due to its tendency to absorb heat.

1876 Campaign Hat

In response to the overwhelming negative comments about the 1872 hat, another board was convened in 1876 to consider among other things "the best pattern of a campaign hat for the Army." After a trial of a hundred proposed new model hats, the Board adopted a new campaign hat constructed of "fine grade" black wool. The brim was two and five-eighths inches on the side and two and one-half inches on the front with a crown that stood five and one-half inches tall. The hat included two of "Brachers' Patent Ventilators" (small metal vent device), one on each side of the crown, three and one-half inches from the brim. This hat was worn with cords and tassels of the pattern prescribed for the 1858 Hardee hat.

The board selected wool over fur felt, even though fur was known to be more durable. The board reasoned that "wool hats of the best grade will give equal service with the best grade of fur hats." However, it later became evident that this was not true, as the wool hats deteriorated at over twice the rate of the fur hats. This decision was clearly driven by cost, as wool hats were one-third the price of hats made from animal fur.

The decision to opt for a black color hat was explained by stating, "For all practical purposes, it is widely believed that black is the most desirable color." On the contrary, recommendations regarding campaign hats had almost universally suggested a light color instead of a dark one, as lighter colors reflect heat while darker colors absorb it. Additionally, the board chose to ignore the compelling 1868 "Woodhull Report" by Assistant Surgeon General Woodhull, which advocated for a lighter-colored hat.

Despite concerns about its durability and color, the 1876 campaign hat proved popular among the troops. Its style resembled John B. Stetson's 1865 "Boss of the Plains" cowboy hat, which was very popular with cowboys and settlers throughout the West. This campaign hat was worn by the U.S. Army from its inception in 1876 until it was replaced by a redesigned version in 1883.

1876 Campaign Hat
Photo Courtesy of Centurion Auctions

Note: The 1876 campaign hat served as the inspiration for the U.S. Army Cavalry hats worn by air cavalry troops during the Vietnam War. Its distinctive size, structure, and color influenced the development of these new cavalry hats, which not only pay homage to their heritage but also remain a vital part of the proud traditions of modern-day cavalry units.

CAMPAIGN HAT REDESIGNED

In early 1882, Assistant Inspector General Major J. C. Breckinridge submitted his report after an extensive tour of frontier posts. He recommended issuing campaign hats of better quality than the current model and suggested the hats be available in either black or drab color, depending on climate.

Upon receiving this report, Brigadier General Rufus Ingalls, the newly appointed quartermaster general, instructed Captain Rogers, the military storekeeper at the Philadelphia Depot, to provide the quartermaster general's office with several sample hats in different colors and qualities. Ingalls noted that the question of whether to issue drab or slate-colored hats had been raised frequently in recent months.

Rogers complied, indicating in his letter of transmittal a decided preference for a change in material and color. "The only proper substance to use in the manufacture of hats of this character," he wrote, "is a fair quality of fur felt." Ingalls selected fur felt hats in the drab color and requested authority to purchase 1,000 hats for test. The hats were identical in design and dimensions to the 1876 campaign hats, with the main differences being their drab color and the use of fur felt material. Unlike the earlier versions, the "Bracher's" metal ventilators were replaced by ventilation holes arranged in a distinctive star pattern, often referred to as "snowflake design."

"DRAB" COLOR

There appears to be no definition of the drab color in the Army regulations. In Brigadier General Ingalls's request for hat prototypes, he mentioned frequent requests for "drab or slate-colored" hats. Woodhull's report recommended a "lighter color" hat and referred to the "pearl or stone color" hats worn by the Second Dragoons in Texas as an example. Another section of Woodhull's report suggested "a gray, light felt hat as the most serviceable and should be fairly tried." Early complaints about the 1858 hat suggested replacing the black hat with a "lightweight gray or dust colored felt hat."

With no specific definition of the drab color, we can infer its shade based on the color of the campaign hats worn by the troops. Most photographs of mounted cavalry soldiers from the late 1800s depict their hats in a medium-brown to tan color. However, there are also photographs that show lighter, possibly stone-colored hats. This color variation can be attributed to various factors, including different manufacturers, dye lots, and the well-known practice of some cavalry soldiers purchasing and customizing store-bought hats.

1883 Campaign Hat

Secretary of War Robert Todd Lincoln (President Lincoln's eldest son) approved Ingalls's request, and 1,000 drab fur hats were procured and distributed to troops stationed in the Southwest. By mid-1883, reports from the field overwhelmingly favored the drab hats. Encouraged by these favorable opinions, Secretary of War Lincoln issued a directive in October 1883, stipulating that only drab fur-felt hats would be procured from that point forward. This directive was well received by the cavalry officers and enlisted soldiers, as the drab campaign hats were cooler, offered protection from the scorching sun, and could be customized in a variety of creative ways.

1883 Campaign Hat
Public Domain Image

7th Cavalry, Fort Laramie, WY – 1889
Public Domain Image

INDIAN WARS

After the Civil War, the westward expansion that began in the 1830s became even more pronounced as settlers were drawn to the opportunity of homesteading in the new territories. During these times, the United States Army acted as the federal government's principal agent of expansion into the western frontier. One historian writes, "At any given time during this period, fewer than 12,000 soldiers occupied the region exceeding 2 million square miles and occupied by some 200,000 Native Americans. Except during major campaigns, the troops remained scattered in units of 50-200 men at more than 100 posts, forts, and cantonments across the frontier."[4]

---

[4] National Cowboy & Western Heritage Museum. "Those Who Served: The U. S. Army on the Frontier - National Cowboy &Amp; Western Heritage Museum," May 9, 2019. https://nationalcowboymuseum.org/explore/served-u-s-army-frontier/.

7th Cavalry, Pine Ridge, SD – 1890
Courtesy of Beinecke Rare Book and Manuscript Library, Yale University

The 1883 campaign hat was versatile and well-suited for the harsh conditions and daily rigors endured by the U.S. Cavalry in the vast expanse of the western frontier. Whether in the cold and snow of the Great Plains or the blazing heat of the desert Southwest, the campaign hat proved to be a reliable companion for cavalry soldiers.

Their continuous use from inception in 1883 until the early years of World War II, with only a slight change in the crown's shape, serves as silent testimony to the campaign hat's utility and soldier preference.[5]

---

[5] Historical information contained in the previous pages attributed to: Howell, Edgar M. 1975. "United States Army Headgear 1855-1902: Catalog of United States Army Uniforms in the Collections of the Smithsonian Institution, II." Smithsonian Studies in History and Technology, (30) 1–109. https://doi.org/10.5479/si.00810258.30.1.

Late 1800s Cavalry Soldier & Horse
Public Domain Image

BUFFALO SOLDIER CAVALRY

After the Civil War in 1866, Congress passed the Army Organization Act, leading to the creation of the 9th and 10th all-Black cavalry regiments. These distinctive cavalry units primarily operated on the western frontier, where their main responsibilities included controlling Native American tribes on the Plains, capturing cattle rustlers, and protecting settlers, stagecoaches, wagon trains, and railroad crews along the frontier.

The mustering of the 9th Cavalry took place in New Orleans, Louisiana, in August and September of 1866 while the 10th Cavalry was headquartered in Fort Leavenworth, Kansas, and mustered the following year. Initially, all-Black regiments were commanded by White officers. It wasn't until the late 1880s that this began to change, as West Point graduates John H. Alexander and Charles Young were granted commissions in the 9th Cavalry.[6]

Both the 9th and 10th Cavalry Regiments took part in numerous skirmishes and larger battles during the Indian Wars as America became increasingly focused on westward expansion. In 1874, the 9th Cavalry was critical to the success of a three-month, unremitting campaign known as the Red River War against the Kiowas, Comanches, Cheyenne, and Arapahoe. Following this conflict, the 10th Cavalry was dispatched to join the 9th Cavalry in Texas.

By 1880, the 9th and 10th Cavalry Regiments had minimized Indian resistance in Texas. The 9th Cavalry was then ordered to Indian Territory, which is now Oklahoma, to prevent White settlers from illegally settling on Indian land. Meanwhile, the 10th Cavalry continued to maintain control over the Apache until the early 1890s, when they were relocated to Montana to apprehend the Cree.

Approximately 20 percent of U.S. Cavalry troops who engaged in the Indian Wars were Buffalo Soldiers, who played a crucial role in at least 177 conflicts.[7]

Early photographs depict Black enlisted troopers wearing forage (Kepi) hats originally issued during the Civil War. This practice continued until the 1883 campaign hat was introduced, as evidenced by a wide range of photos taken in the mid- to late 1880s showing the Buffalo Soldiers wearing the drab color campaign hat.

---

[6] Texas State Historical Association. n.d. "The History of the Ninth Cavalry: A Legacy of the Buffalo Soldiers." https://www.tshaonline.org/handbook/entries/ninth-united-states-cavalry.

[7] HISTORY.com Editors. 2025. "Buffalo Soldiers - Definition, Logo & Facts | HISTORY." HISTORY. February 27, 2025. https://www.history.com/articles/buffalo-soldiers.

(l to r) PVT James Satchel and PVT Samuel Tipton
Troop C, 9th Cavalry, 1891
Public Domain Image

9th Cavalry – Buffalo Soldiers Wearing 1883 Campaign Hats
Camp Lawton, WA, 1900
Courtesy University of Washington Special Collections

Teddy Roosevelt and the Rough Riders

Among Theodore Roosevelt's numerous lifetime accomplishments, few resonate as powerfully as his military service as a "Rough Rider" during the Spanish-American War. In the 1890s, America's attention turned to Cuba's quest for liberation, driven by compelling media accounts that exposed the abuses of Spanish rule. Roosevelt emerged as one of the most ardent champions of Cuban independence. In his role as assistant secretary of the Navy, he not only fervently advocated for military action against Spain but also took decisive steps to prepare the Navy for battle.

On February 15, 1898, the battleship USS *Maine*, anchored in Havana Harbor, suddenly exploded, killing 262 American sailors. Spain firmly denied any involvement in the explosion of the USS *Maine*; however, a U.S. Navy investigation determined that a mine was responsible. While the exact cause of the explosion remains a mystery, American journalists and Assistant Secretary of the Navy Theodore Roosevelt were adamant that it constituted an act of war by Spain. This overwhelming sentiment ultimately paved the way for the declaration of war.

An enthusiastic Roosevelt resigned from his position as assistant secretary of the Navy and requested permission from the secretary of war to form a volunteer regiment. Although he had three years of experience as a National Guard captain, Roosevelt deferred the regiment's leadership to Leonard Wood, a war hero and trusted friend. With Wood, as colonel, and Roosevelt, as lieutenant colonel, they began recruiting and organizing the 1st U.S. Volunteer Cavalry.

Roosevelt's charisma and larger-than-life personality swiftly positioned him as the undisputed leader of a remarkable coalition of polo players, hunters, cowboys, Native Americans, and spirited college athletes. The legendary cavalry regiment became known as "Roosevelt's Rough Riders."

Every member of the Rough Riders was equipped with a horse and outfitted in tan cotton uniforms, a practical alternative to the traditional woolen attire. They donned the iconic 1883 campaign hat, and most soldiers were armed with the latest pistols, rifles, and a sturdy Bowie knife.[8]

During the ten-week war, the Rough Riders participated in two important battles. The first was the Battle of Las Guasimas on June 24. In this battle, the Spanish forces were defeated when Roosevelt led a flanking assault, causing them to retreat.

The second, and undoubtedly more significant, action was the Battle of San Juan Hill, which took place on July 1. Roosevelt described it as "the great day of my life." He led a series of charges up Kettle Hill toward San Juan Hill while riding his horse, Texas, with the Rough Riders following on foot.

> **Note:** There was general chaos and disorganization in Tampa, Florida, as the Rough Riders were about to embark to Cuba. Due to a lack of storage on the ships assigned for the journey, many horses – and some men – had to be left behind. As a result, the troopers fought on foot, with the exception of Teddy Roosevelt, who managed to get a single horse onto the shore in Cuba.[9]

---

[8] Wood-Davis, Kelley. 2011. "The Real Story of the Rough Riders." HubPages. October 11, 2011. Accessed May 3, 2025. https://discover.hubpages.com/education/The-Real-Story-of-the-Rough-Riders.

[9] Anderberg, Jeremy. 2021. "Outfitted & Equipped in History: American Rough Rider." The Art of Manliness. June 17, 2021. https://www.artofmanliness.com/character/military/outfitted-equipped-american-rough-rider/.

Roosevelt rode up and down the hill, encouraging his men with commands to "March!" During the battle, he fired a revolver that he salvaged from the *Maine*, killing one Spaniard. Other regiments fought alongside him, and eventually, the American flag was raised over San Juan Hill.[10]

The war had profound and enduring impacts. Roosevelt emerged from the conflict as a celebrated war hero, capturing the nation's admiration. Three short years after his triumphant charge at San Juan Hill, he rode into the White House, embodying the spirit of a new America, ready to assert its influence on the world stage. At the same time, the Rough Riders Volunteer Cavalry etched their legacy into history, forever remembered for their bravery and fortitude.

COL Theodore Roosevelt – 1898
Wearing 1883 Campaign Hat
Courtesy Library of Congress

---

[10] "T. R. the Rough Rider: Hero of the Spanish American War - Theodore Roosevelt Birthplace National Historic Site (U.S. National Park Service)." n.d. https://www.nps.gov/thrb/learn/historyculture/tr-rr-spanamwar.htm.

Teddy Roosevelt and the Rough Riders at San Juan Hill – July 1898
Courtesy Library of Congress

CAVALRY MOVIES

The romanticized image of the U.S. Cavalry in the late 1800s was a popular theme for movie producers during the 1950s and 1960s. Among them, John Ford stood out as a master director and producer, dedicated to achieving unmatched historical accuracy in his films. By meticulously recreating cavalry uniforms, horse tack, and weaponry, he masterfully brought these stories to life, offering visually stunning and authentic representations of the U.S. Cavalry.

Filmed on location in Monument Valley, John Ford's cavalry films prominently showcased the lighter-colored 1883 campaign hat, highlighting it as the essential "working hat" for the horse cavalry during their battles against the Indians. This attention to detail not only captivates the audience but also honors the rich history of the cavalry.

Ford's most famous cavalry movies – *Rio Grande, Fort Apache,* and *She Wore a Yellow Ribbon* – came to be known as the Cavalry Trilogy. In each of these captivating movies, John Wayne takes center stage as the quintessential cavalry soldier, embodying the bravery and honor of the era. These films not only showcase Wayne's remarkable talent but also celebrate the spirit of the American West, making them essential viewing for anyone who appreciates classic cinema and the legacy of the cavalry.

John Wayne and Ben Johnson
Wearing 1883 Campaign Hats
She Wore a Yellow Ribbon, directed by John Ford, 1949
Argosy Pictures – RKO

Rex Gooch

PART 2
THE CALVARY HAT

CHAPTER 3

BIRTH OF THE CAV HAT

TESTING THE AIR CAVALRY CONCEPT

On March 19, 1964, 3rd Squadron of the 17th Cavalry was activated at Fort Benning, Georgia, as part of the 11th Air Assault Division. Their mission was to validate the air cavalry concept using helicopters for combat air assaults and troop movement. Throughout the following months, the 3rd of the 17th Cavalry experienced a whirlwind of rigorous developmental testing

11th Air Assault Division
Courtesy Army Aviation Magazine

while living in the field and participating in one tactical exercise after another.

By November 15, 1964, the tests had been completed, and the Army had approved the airmobile concept. On July 3, 1965, the 11th Air Assault Division was renamed the 1st Cavalry Division (Airmobile). As part of this change, the 3rd of the 17th Cavalry was inactivated and redesignated as the 1st of the 9th Cavalry. This marked the birth of the airmobile concept and the air cavalry.

At the same time, the division was put on alert for deployment overseas to the Republic of Vietnam, which occurred ninety days later on September 15, 1965.

Origination of the Cavalry Hat

In early 1964, Lieutenant Colonel John B. Stockton assumed command of the newly activated 3rd Squadron, 17th Cavalry. He named this new unit the "Bullwhip Squadron" to instill a sense of pride and embody the spirit of swift and decisive action. Under Stockton's command, the groundbreaking air cavalry concept was developed and rigorously tested during the 1964 field trials.

Stockton was known for his no-nonsense, highly professional, and innovative approach to flying and fighting. His unwavering dedication and visionary leadership earned him profound respect and admiration from the troopers who proudly served under his command.[11]

In November 1964, following the successful completion of the field trials, Lieutenant Colonel Stockton began wearing the first modern-day black cavalry hat, a gift from his cavalry troopers. This distinctive hat swiftly emerged as the preferred

---

[11] Ewart, LTC (Ret) Loel. October 6, 2007. Speech at dedication of the Vietnam section of the Motts Military Museum.

headgear for the 3rd Squadron troopers, significantly boosting their morale and camaraderie. As a result, Lieutenant Colonel Stockton is often referred to as the "Father of the Cavalry Hat."

LTC John B. Stockton,
Commander, 1st of the 9th Cavalry, 1965
Courtesy 1st Cavalry Division Association

CAVALRY HAT BACKSTORY

You might be curious: "Who had the vision to create the very first cavalry hat?" The answer dates back to 1964, when the Bullwhip Squadron conducted intensive developmental testing of air assault and air cavalry concepts. It was during this time that two spirited and innovative captains collaborated to create a cavalry hat inspired by the 1876 campaign hat worn by the horse cavalry.

After a period of intensive simulated combat training in North and South Carolina, members of the squadron were authorized several days of well-deserved rest and recreation (R&R) on a staggered schedule. Captains Walt Harmon and Bill Gillette took this opportunity to return to Fort Benning, Georgia, to reunite with their wives.

Walt, who arrived a couple of days ahead of Bill, visited the Fort Benning salvage store, where he found olive drab, Montana-peak drill sergeant hats for sale. Having purchased several of these hats, Walt and Bill met to plan the transformation into proper cavalry hats. It didn't take long for the two cavalry captains to decide that the motley specimens had three problems: the color of the hats, the shape of the hats, and the necessary hat cords to designate general officers, commissioned officers, warrant officers, and enlisted troopers.

The color issue was resolved when the two resourceful cavalry troopers convinced their wives that black dye could easily turn their hats black. However, this task proved to be more complicated than it initially seemed. It required several dyeing attempts before their hats achieved the desired color, and, of course, the dye pot boiled over in the kitchen a couple of times.

In Phenix City, Alabama, across the Chattahoochee River, the officers found a shop that agreed to steam and shape their hats as prescribed. Unsure how to address the issue of hat cords, they conducted a reconnaissance of Columbus, Georgia. In the city's back alleys, they discovered the owner of a secondhand shop who had a drawer full of hat cords and was unsure of what to do with them. A deal was quickly made, and they were able to create several examples of what would become the black cavalry hat.

Upon reaching the end of their R&R, Walt and Bill reported back to the squadron assembly area on the banks of

Wateree Pond in South Carolina. After returning to their troop area, they realized they needed to find a way to gain acceptance of the black cavalry hats. After some discussion, they concluded, "What better way to gain acceptance than to honor our squadron commander with a gift of one of the hats?" They decided to present Lieutenant Colonel Stockton with a black cavalry hat on his upcoming birthday.[12]

LTC STOCKTON'S BIRTHDAY PRESENT

Stockton wrote:

> As it happened, the last day of rest (R&R) was also my 42nd birthday. Ever alert, Command Sergeant Major Kennedy got with his network of sources in the squadron and came up with the idea of an impromptu surprise birthday celebration.
>
> Kennedy lured me into the command post (CP) trailer for some purpose and kept me there talking for about half an hour. When I poked my head outside, it seemed that maybe half the squadron had gathered in virtual silence around the CP trailer.
>
> Looming out of the crowd was Bill Gillette, wearing the crudest World War I campaign hat known to man. It was kind of a slimy gray/green mottled color, the sweatband was virtually rotted out, and there was much evidence that moths had been hard at work on the felt for many years. With full ceremony, young Gillette presented me this monstrosity on behalf of his fellow Troopers.

---

[12] Gillette, LTC (Ret) Bill. March 2011. "From the Waterdee to the Pee Dee." *Bullwhip Squadron Association Newsletter*.

Strangely enough, for I have a long and narrow size 7 1/2 head, the old campaign hat fit me almost perfectly. I promptly put it on and suffered through the rest of my birthday surprise. Just as we were breaking up to get back to duty there was a flurry of activity out on the edge of the dispersing crowd, and who should heave into view but the Division Commanding General himself, then-Brigadier General Harry Kinnard, in living color. I reported to him immediately, forgetful of my headgear. That was my first but far from my last run-in with military authorities about black hat wearing.[13]

Note: LTC Stockton's original Cav Hat is on display at the National Mounted Warrior Museum at Fort Hood, Texas. This campaign hat, originally dyed black, has faded to dark brown over the years.

LTC John B. Stockton's Hat
Courtesy National Mounted Warrior
Museum at Fort Hood, TX

LTC (Ret) Bill Gillette
Wearing His Dyed Campaign Hat
Courtesy 1st Cavalry Division Association

---

[13] Chole, Bert. 2000. "The Stuff of Which Legends are Born." *2000 Bullwhip Squadron Reunion Booklet.*

NEW SOURCE FOR CAVALRY HATS

The procurement of cavalry hats went smoothly; however, by early spring 1965, the supply of salvage hats at Fort Benning had been exhausted. This was a welcome relief for the wives who were enduring hat dyeing in their kitchens.

Despite ongoing procurement challenges, the demand for cavalry hats increased dramatically. This escalating situation necessitated another planning meeting to strategize future hat procurement. Walt Harman and Bill Gillette surmised that since the John B. Stetson Hat Company name was stamped on the leather sweatband of some of the salvage hats, they might be able to supply the new cavalry hats. Bill took a picture of his hat and sent it to the Stetson Hat Company in St. Joseph, Missouri, along with their request. The response was immediate and outstanding: the Stetson sales manager agreed to supply the prescribed hat together with appropriate hat cord at a reasonable price. Thus, the foundation was laid for the revival of the 1876 campaign hat – now called "The Cavalry Hat."

YOU CAN'T WEAR THAT HERE

As Bill Gillette noted, "the story of the reinstitution of the black cavalry hat would be incomplete if some of the earlier wearing difficulties were not included," so he concluded his account as follows.

As the squadron's hats became increasingly visible at Fort Benning, our Division Commander, Major General Kinnard, became more forceful in his objections to the wearing of cavalry hats. Not desiring to irritate our commander, we became very careful where we wore our hats. They were essentially relegated to wear in the field and the squadron area at Harmony Church (which was almost in the field). All went well until the squadron conducted a counter-insurgency exercise at Camp Shelby, Mississippi. Being in the field, we wore our cavalry hats. Evidently, while there, a news photographer took a picture of members of the squadron wearing black cavalry hats. The aftermath of the Camp Shelby publicity took place at Fort Benning one Sunday morning several weeks later.

That was the day Lieutenant Colonel Stockton picked up the telephone and heard the following from the Army Chief of Staff: "Colonel, this is General Johnson. Don't you believe in the uniform I have prescribed for the Army?"[14]

THE FIRST CAVALRY ARRIVES IN VIETNAM

The 1st Squadron, 9th Cavalry Division officially arrived in Vietnam in September 1965, although some soldiers had arrived earlier. Initially, the cavalry troopers, known for their distinctive black hats, faced significant opposition from key members of the Division's chain of command, who insisted on a return to the authorized headgear. However, as the battles escalated and the war intensified, higher command became preoccupied with more urgent matters. And cavalry units were often operating in remote areas, far from the higher command that might have objected to the unauthorized headwear.

Slowly but surely, cavalry troopers boldly and confidently wore their cavalry hats without fear of reprimand. And, frankly, some of the "crustier" troopers didn't care about potential reprimand. The oft-heard phrase was: "What's the worst they can do? Send me to Vietnam?"

---

[14] Gillette, LTC (Ret) Bill. March 2011. "From the Waterdee to the Pee Dee." *Bullwhip Squadron Association Newsletter*.

As the "tradition" evolved, the distinctive black hat became a symbol of pride and unity in the air cavalry, and it wasn't long before air cavalry troops throughout Vietnam adopted this proud tradition. As its popularity grew, the cavalry hat eventually became known as the "Cav Hat."

CAVALRY STETSONS IN VIETNAM

Because the source of the cavalry hat was the Stetson Hat Company, the name "Stetson" became synonymous with the Cav Hat in Vietnam, and many troopers referred to their hat as their "Stetson." This high-quality hat was available for private purchase and had a hefty price tag of $17.50 in 1971.

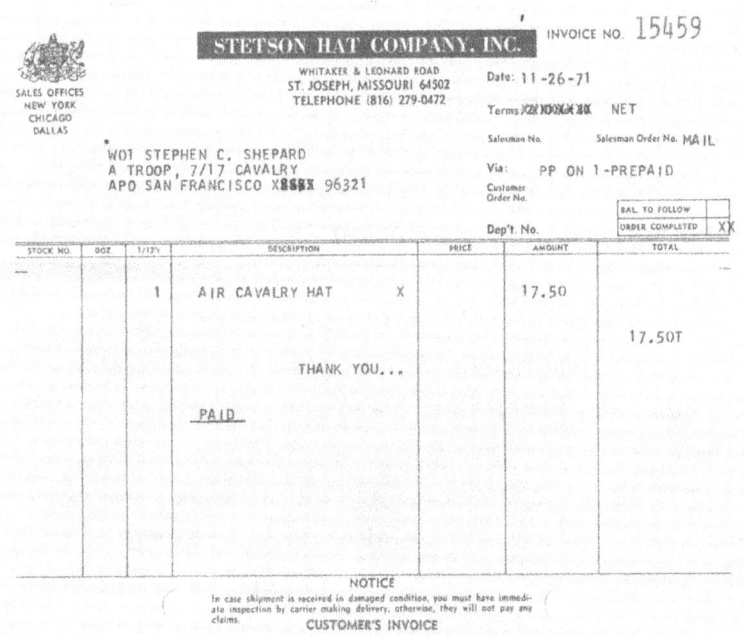

Stetson Cav Hat Receipt – 1971
WO1 Steve Shepard, C/7/17 & H/10
Image Courtesy of John Conway, Legacy of Valor

Calvary Stetsons were crafted from quality beaver, rabbit, or wild hare fur. The hats featured an interior leather sweatband and a silk hat ribbon encircling the base of the crown. The brim was three inches wide, and the crown stood four and three-quarter inches tall. Grommets located in the brim above each ear served as pass-throughs for a black leather chin strap, which was worn draped around the back of the neck.

The hat cord was modeled after the acorn-ended cords worn on the 1876 campaign hat. During the Vietnam War, there appeared to be no color guidelines for these cords. The colors provided by Stetson were as follows: officers, gold cords; warrant officers, silver cords; and enlisted personnel, yellow cords made of either wool or nylon.

> **Note:** In the years following the Vietnam War, cord color guidelines were defined as: general officers, all gold braid; officers, gold and black intertwined braid; warrant officers, silver and black intertwined braid; enlisted, yellow wool or nylon.

Most officers and warrant officers wore some combination of officer rank insignia and shiny brass crossed cavalry sabers on the front crown of their hats. Some cavalry troopers embellished their hats with distinctive hat pins on either side of the crown, like the iconic coiled cobra pin. The Stetsons were remarkably durable and were easily cleaned of dirt and lint by buffing with a stiff brush.

Although troop commanders did not mandate the wearing of cavalry hats, there was significant peer pressure to adopt the cavalry spirit. As a result, most troopers ordered their hats soon after joining the unit. Typically, one individual within the troop was designated to collect the names, ranks, hat sizes, and payments before placing an order with Stetson. In Phu Loi, the squadron chaplain handled the orders for the troopers of the 3rd of the 17th Air Cavalry.

The hats were shipped from the Stetson manufacturing plant in Missouri, which resulted in a turnaround time of several weeks between ordering and delivery. In some cases, soldiers were killed in action or medevaced to the United States before their hats arrived. Consequently, some soldiers ended up receiving hats that had originally been intended for their fallen or wounded comrades.

Stetson Cavalry Hat
Photo Courtesy of CavHooah

The Cav Hat served as a morale booster and fostered a strong sense of pride and loyalty among the units where it was worn. By the cessation of hostilities, virtually all air cavalry (and some ground cavalry) units had adopted the Cav Hat.[15]

---

[15] Johnson, Lawrence H. III. 1990. *Winged Sabers*. Stackpole Books.

CAVALRY PRIDE

Cavalry pilots and crewmembers often experienced an exhilarating adrenaline rush from flying combat missions. After a demanding day in the skies, it was customary for air cavalry troopers, wearing their distinctive Cav Hats, to gather at the officers' club. There, they would revel in their triumphs and unwind from the rigors of the day with oftentimes outrageous celebrations.

Amidst the revelry, troopers frequently belted out cavalry songs along with crude renditions of popular tunes. The atmosphere was filled with vibrant energy and exuberant laughter. It is likely that during these festivities, the iconic phrase "If you ain't Cav, you ain't sh*t!" first took root, embodying the bold pride and camaraderie of those who served in "The Cav."

VIETNAM CAV HAT STORIES

The following chapter shares unique stories about Cav Hats and the troopers who proudly wore this distinctive headgear during the Vietnam War. The stories shared by individuals may use unfamiliar terms and locations. If you encounter any unknown terminology or places, please consult the following appendices at the rear of this book.

>Appendix I: Vietnam Cav Hat Stories Terminology
>Appendix II: South Vietnam Map of Story Locations

CHAPTER 4
VIETNAM CAV HAT STORIES

"MY CAV HAT TOOK HITS"

Cavalry pilots frequently carried their Cav Hats with them when flying combat missions in South Vietnam. The following story recounts how a cavalry hat became a combat casualty.

In 1971, B Troop, 1st of the 9th Air Cavalry, was stationed at Bearcat Base, approximately thirty-three klicks due east of Tan Son Nhut Airbase in Saigon. The troop callsign was "Saber."

Early morning on the 25th of April 1971, Captain Dick Cross, scout platoon leader with callsign Saber White 16, is performing a preflight inspection on his OH-6A scout helicopter positioned inside a sandbag revetment alongside the Bearcat Army Airfield. Upon completing the inspection, Dick removes his Cav Hat and places it behind the anti-torque pedals, against the Plexiglass bubble windscreen. Then, Cross climbs into the right-side pilot's seat while his door gunner, Specialist 4th Class Woodham, known by all as "Woody," climbs into the rear compartment of the OH-6A. After starting his aircraft, Dick brings the scout helicopter to a hover and taxies to the runway, joining an AH-1G Cobra gunship. After calling the tower for clearance, the two helicopters take off in a south-southwesterly direction.

THE MISSION

Today's operation is a hunter-killer mission, about six to eight klicks south of Bearcat, where an enemy force is known to be operating. Upon their arrival at the area of operations, Dick flies at treetop level, scouting along a small river while the Cobra gunship flies at a higher altitude, covering the small scout helicopter below.

Dick and Woody carefully scan the dense woods alongside the river, their eyes sharp and focused, on the lookout for any signs of enemy activity. After some time of finding nothing of consequence, Dick comes upon a series of bunkers dug into the hillside overlooking the river. The bunkers appear to have been used recently but show no evidence of activity today. After being on station for almost two hours, the team returns to Bearcat for refueling.

Upon returning to the operations area, Cross revisits the bunkers and, to his surprise, encounters a large enemy force lying in wait. Apparently, the refueling interval gave the enemy ample time to set a trap. In an instant, the enemy unleashes a barrage of automatic weapons fire, and Dick hears the dreaded pinging sound of bullets ripping through the thin aluminum skin of his aircraft. With adrenaline pumping, Cross rapidly banks to the right to evade the gunfire. By some stroke of luck, none of the enemy rounds found their mark on Cross, and in a critical, life-or-death moment, Dick instinctively pulls in power to make a swift escape from the enemy's firing zone.

"Woody, Are You Okay?"

After evading the enemy and despite smoke billowing from the engine compartment, Captain Cross determines the aircraft is still flyable, even though the torque gauge is missing and the rotor RPM indicator needle rests soundly on zero. A hurried check of the radios reveals that only the FM tactical radio is functioning. Using the still-working intercom, Dick calls his door gunner and says, "Woody, are you okay?" Woodham replies, "I'm hit." Dick turns to look at Woody in the rear seat and discovers Woodham's face is covered in blood, bleeding from shards of broken Plexiglass impacting his face.

Filled with concern for Woody's injuries, Cross banks his aircraft toward Bearcat and increases the airspeed to an urgent 90 knots. Realizing that the crippled aircraft's engine may fail at any moment, Dick flies the stricken aircraft back to Bearcat with great trepidation. Using the FM radio, Cross calls Saber Troop Operations Center and tells them his door gunner is wounded and requests an ambulance be ready on the flight line.

"I Cut Off a Chinook"

Upon arriving at the airfield, Cross ignores the standard traffic pattern and rapidly descends toward the runway, narrowly cutting off a Chinook helicopter on final approach. After briefly coming to a hover over the tarmac, Dick taxies directly to the Saber area on the runway apron and sets his OH-6A down among other Saber helicopters, where he immediately shuts down the turbine engine.

While the rotor blades are winding down, an ambulance pulls alongside the Loach, and two medics rush to assist Woody in the right-side rear compartment. The medics carefully extract Woodham from the Loach, place him on a stretcher, and rush him to the open rear doors of the ambulance. After securing the stretcher inside the ambulance, the medics jump aboard and pull the doors closed as the ambulance races off to the infirmary.

TWENTY-SIX BULLET HOLES

Then, as the rotor blades slow to a near stop, Dick unbuckles his seat belt/shoulder harness and climbs out of the aircraft. While walking around his helicopter to perform a postflight inspection, Cross is astonished by what he sees. There are twenty-six bullet holes in his aircraft, including one large hole in the tail boom and a hit on the forward edge of one of the tail rotor blades. The crippled aircraft is leaking fuel and oil into a large pool beneath the helicopter. It's a miracle that this aircraft was able to return to Bearcat.

At some point, Cross reaches into the cockpit to retrieve his Cav Hat from behind the pedals and is surprised to find it has two bullet holes, one in the top of the crown and the other in the brim. In addition to Woody's injuries and the heavy damage to his helicopter, another casualty of this mission is Dick's cherished cavalry hat.

The following photos were taken by Chief Warrant Officer 2 Roger Cox, Saber 18, who happened to have his camera handy when Cross was inspecting his bullet-ridden aircraft. Look closely and you can see Dick's finger sticking through the bullet hole in the crown of his Cav Hat.

Captain Dick Cross – Bullet Holes in Cav Hat
Photo Courtesy of Roger Cox

Captain Dick Cross – Bullet Holes in Tail Boom and Tail Rotor
Photo Courtesy of Roger Cox

After securing his aircraft, Captain Cross walks to the infirmary to check on Woody. There he learns that Woodham has a bullet wound in his leg and another in his arm. After applying bandages and treating his facial lacerations, the medical team arranges for Woody to be medevaced to an evacuation hospital for further treatment.

At some point, one of the medics turns his attention to Dick, saying, "Captain Cross, how are you?" Dick replies, "Oh, I'm fine, no injuries." The medic starts to inspect Cross from head to toe when he sees blood on the backside of Dick's left trouser leg. After placing Cross on the examination table, they find several pieces of shrapnel imbedded in the back of Dick's calf. Using a scalpel and tweezers, the Medic removes the small fragments of aircraft metal from his leg. Sometime later, Captain Cross learns that both he and Specialist 4th Class Woodham are recipients of Purple Hearts.

"I Wanna Be a Scout Pilot"

After graduating from U.S. Army Flight School in 1970, Warrant Officer Michael Goff received his orders for Vietnam. On the long overseas flight, Mike met and became friends with Captain Olan Howe, also a recent graduate of Army flight school.

After reporting into the 90th Replacement Battalion at Long Binh, both Mike and Olan learn they are assigned to B Troop, 2nd of the 17th Air Cavalry, operating out of Camp Eagle in I Corps.

After arriving at Camp Eagle and settling into their new surroundings, the two friends make their way to an O-Club situated on a small hill overlooking the bustling airfield and a PSP landing pad below. While there, the two aviators enjoy a drink, listen to air traffic broadcasts over the bar's loudspeaker, and observe the activity on the flight line.

"Nobody Messes with the Scouts"

During their conversation, Captain Howe informs Goff of his intention to become a scout pilot and possibly scout platoon leader. Howe explains, "Nobody messes with the scouts because they are all volunteers, and they don't fly at night or in bad weather because of the 'Mickey Mouse' instruments in the Loach." Howe's passion for flying scouts is not only contagious but also compelling, and his reasoning resonates strongly with Goff.

A short time later, Mike and Olan watch out the window to observe an OH-6A scout helicopter flying low and fast toward their location. The small aircraft flares to a hover and sets down at the bottom of the hill leading up to the O-Club. Watching as the rotor blades slow to a stop, they see the scout pilot remove his helmet, exit the Loach, and reach back inside the cockpit to retrieve his helmet bag. Reaching inside the bag, the pilot pulls out a well-worn black cavalry hat. After giving it a few firm slaps against his trouser leg to remove the dust, he places it on his head. Then, with the confident stride of a cavalryman, he walks up the hill to the O-Club to order a burger and Coke.

Mike, impressed by the image of this bold scout pilot wearing a striking black cavalry hat, thinks, *I wanna be a scout pilot*. Later, Goff and Howe eagerly volunteer to be scouts, ready to embrace the challenges and dangers that lie ahead.

Since Mike had no experience in the scout helicopter, Olan made arrangements for Mike to attend the weeklong OH-6A transition school at Vung Tau. After completing his training, Mike returns to B Troop and is shocked to learn that Captain Olan Howe was killed when his helicopter was shot down during an orientation flight in the A Shau Valley. Mike is devastated; his first in-country friend is killed, and, for a time, this tragedy serves to fuel the uncertainty of what lies ahead.

"I Flew with the Best"

In the coming months, Goff becomes a seasoned and respected scout pilot with the callsign Banshee 12. Years later Mike commented, "I was fortunate. I flew with and became close friends with some of the finest pilots and bravest patriots I have ever known. I always felt my serving as a Banshee scout pilot was a tribute to the legacy of my good friend, Captain Olan Howe."

Shortly after joining the scout platoon, Mike received his long-awaited cavalry hat. He proudly attached his warrant officer rank and the 2-17 Cavalry crossed sabers to the front of the crown. Around the base of the crown, he added a colorful, beaded Indian hat band. Occasionally, he further embellished his cavalry hat with a feather tucked into the hat band.

This striking hat band was created by Goff's sister. The design and colors were inspired by the Miccosukee Indian tribe, one of three recognized Seminole entities whose homeland is in the Everglades, not far from where Michael grew up. Unfortunately, Mike's Cav Hat did not make it back to the States on his return trip. Years later, Goff ordered a new Stetson to recreate his original hat, as shown below. He proudly wears his Cav Hat to helicopter pilot reunions and other veteran events.

Mike Goff's Cav Hat
Photo Courtesy of Mike Goff

A Purple Heart for My Cav Hat

During the 1972 Easter Offensive, F Troop, 4th Air Cavalry was stationed at Tan My Army Airfield, located near the coast of South Vietnam in I Corps. F Troop's nickname and callsign was "Centaur." At that time, F Troop was the northernmost American Army unit, and its area of operations (AO) bordered the demilitarized zone (DMZ) on the north.

The Mission

In early June of 1972, First Lieutenant Russ Miller, callsign Centaur 47, was the aircraft commander of an AH-1G Cobra gunship. He was part of a five-aircraft reconnaissance team that includes two Cobras, two Loaches, and a single Slick serving as the command and control (C&C) aircraft. Their mission was to search for and identify the advancing North Vietnamese Army (NVA) and report on their disposition. The area of operation was located west of Highway 1 and just north of the river that divides Quang Tri from Thua Thien Province. The terrain was characterized by high, steep-sided hills and narrow valleys, all covered by dense, triple-canopy jungle.

Using established Centaur low-level tactics to evade enemy heat-seeking missiles, the two OH-6A scout helicopters suddenly came under heavy enemy fire from beneath the jungle canopy. As the scouts exited the area, one of the Loach gunners tossed a smoke grenade to mark the enemy's location. Upon hearing the scout pilots call, "Taking Fire," the two Cobra helicopters began a series of low-level, pop-up gun runs, firing rockets and minigun rounds into the area marked by the smoke.

"47 Is Hit!"

After several gun runs, Russ Miller comes on the radio, excitedly announcing, "47 is hit," and after a pause, he adds, "47 is going down." This frantic announcement comes immediately after three large .51-caliber bullets rip through Russ's gunship. Flying the lead Loach, First Lieutenant Frank Walker responds, "We're right with you, 47," as the two scouts close in on the disabled Cobra.

Realizing that a forced landing in the dense jungle could be fatal, Miller quickly reevaluates his situation and decides to make every effort to keep his crippled aircraft in the air.

After exiting the valley, the Cav team of four helicopters, with Russ in the lead, locates Highway 1 and proceeds south to Camp Evans, thinking Russ can land on the highway if forced to go down. During the flight, Russ radios that his main rotor caution light is illuminated. This is a serious issue, as a transmission seizure could cause the helicopter to drop like a brick. First Lieutenant Pete Holmberg, flying the trail Loach, flies beneath Russ's gunship and confirms a transmission leak; the belly of the gunship is coated with transmission fluid. With no loss of main rotor RPM, Miller decides to risk continuing the flight to Camp Evans.

Glad to Be Alive

Flying the disabled gunship is a tense and nerve-wracking experience for Miller, but he ultimately manages to reach Camp Evans, where he quickly lands and shuts down the aircraft's turbine engine. As the main rotor blades slowly turn to a halt, the Cav team members gather around Russ's Cobra and are astonished by what they see. The main rotor transmission has a half-inch crack running from top to bottom and has leaked almost all its transmission fluid. Additionally, a .51-caliber bullet pierced the fuselage from the lower left, passing behind Miller's head. It shattered the shelf behind the aircraft commander's seat before exiting through the pilot's canopy, creating a large two-by-three-foot hole in the Plexiglass.

Like most air cavalry gunship pilots, Russ had placed his prized cavalry hat on the shelf behind his head. Sadly, his hat became a casualty of war when the .51-caliber bullet struck it, ripping through and obliterating the right side of the brim.

In a miraculous turn of events, Russ narrowly escaped serious injury and skillfully saved his aircraft, while his Cav Hat undoubtedly deserved a Purple Heart.

Shortly after landing at Camp Evans, the following photo captured Miller wearing a "Glad to be alive" smile.

1LT Russ Miller
His Cav Hat Hit by a .51-Caliber Bullet
Photo Courtesy of centaursinvietnam.org

Note: On July 11, 1972, First Lieutenant Russ Miller was the recipient of the Distinguished Flying Cross for his role in the "Rescue of Lady Ace," a daring nighttime rescue of six surviving crewmembers of a U.S. Marine CH-53D helicopter shot down by an SA-7 heat-seeking missile three klicks north-northeast of Quang Tri.[16]

---

[16] Gooch, Rex. 2014. "The Rescue of Lady Ace." *Flight Journal*, December. Volume 20, No. 6.

"My Cav Hat Was Kidnapped by the Marines"

In January 1972, Captain Mike Henry arrived in Vietnam for his second tour of duty. He was assigned to D Troop, 229th Assault Helicopter Battalion, stationed at Bien Hoa Airbase, where he was designated the Gun Platoon leader. D Troop operated as an air cavalry unit as part of the Garry Owen Task Force and was the last remaining element of the 1st Cavalry Division in Vietnam. The troop's callsign was "Smiling Tigers," and their patches proudly displayed a cartoonish, vibrant orange tiger with an ear-to-ear smile.

Smiling Tigers Insignia
Designed by Walt Disney Studios in 1967
This design was requested by one of the D Troopers

1972 Easter Offensive

The first three months of 1972 were relatively calm in comparison to previous times, leading some to speculate that the war was winding down. However, this notion quickly disappeared with the onset of the Easter Offensive in 1972. During this military operation, multiple divisions of the North Vietnamese

Army (NVA) launched massive attacks into South Vietnam from Laos and Cambodia and across the Demilitarized Zone (DMZ). The NVA conducted an aggressive ground offensive, utilizing Russian tanks and advanced anti-aircraft weaponry, which included .51- and .37-caliber anti-aircraft guns, as well as shoulder-fired Strela heat-seeking missiles.

U.S. Air Cavalry troops were at the forefront of this battle, charged with the mission to turn back the tide of NVA aggressor forces. The battle raged on for several months, with pilots and crewmembers flying day after day with little time for rest. The combat missions were challenging, dangerous, and inherently risky, causing tensions to run extremely high.

THE CHOIR

In these challenging times, Smiling Tiger pilots would gather in the troops' makeshift officers' club after a grueling day in the skies. Here, they could unwind, releasing the stress of combat and briefly forgetting the dangers they faced. This often led to an evening of drinking, carousing, and camaraderie. In the midst of this spirited revelry, a group called "The Choir" was formed, and its role was to add singing to the merriment. Led by the choir director, Captain Paul (Bimbo) Lent, the melodious group was composed of Captain Ernest C. (Buzz) Johnson, First Lieutenant Dave Wallace, Chief Warrant Officer 2 Mike (The Perch Man) Syverson, and several others.

Having leadership responsibility for the Gun platoon and also being a member of The Choir, Captain Henry commented, "Because I have always considered myself a Christian, I encouraged The Choir to sing songs of a more soothing nature, such as old and comfortable gospel songs; but no, The Choir insisted on singing calloused and insensitive hymns. What was I to do? Such a leadership conundrum."

The Smiling Tigers' base of operations was situated on the southern side of Bien Hoa Airbase, a major aviation complex, located twenty-five klicks northwest of Saigon. This airbase was capable of accommodating both large fixed-wing and rotor-wing aircraft, as well as meeting the needs of fighter jets.

On the northern side of the airbase, the Air Force and Navy personnel enjoyed a higher standard of living compared to the Army. They had nearby access to the officers' club, a post exchange, and considerably better food. Occasionally, the Smiling Tigers would travel by deuce-and-a-half truck, with a designated driver, to the officers' club for meals, entertainment, socializing, and much-needed stress relief.

The Marines – Tomcats

One evening in early summer 1972, following an intense day of combat flight operations, the Smiling Tigers were transported to the Bien Hoa officers' club for a night of socializing with Marine Corps and Air Force aviators who frequented this club. It was on this night that the Smiling Tigers faced off with Marine Fighter Attack Squadron VMA-311, known as "The Tomcats." This Marine Corps aviation unit flew the A-4 Skyhawk, a single-engine jet aircraft utilized for attack purposes.

The Tomcat Marine aviators turned out to be just as rowdy, aggressive, and spirited as their counterparts, the Smiling Tigers. As the night went on, the aviators escalated the friendly competition between the rival services with loud banter, plenty of drinks, and the kind of wild antics that only young men in a dangerous combat zone can come up with.

As the night of festivities reached its peak, The Choir decided to serenade the Tomcats. After a series of raunchy, humorous songs and plenty of laughter, the rowdy aviators gathered their belongings to leave. It was at that moment that Captain Henry realized his prized Cav Hat was missing.

"WHERE'S THE CAV HAT?"

After a quick search, it became clear that one of the A-4 pilots had snatched the hat. At that point, the assistant choir director, Captain Buzz Johnson, pulled out his .45-caliber handgun and fired two rounds into the ceiling while shouting, "Where's the Cav Hat?" The bar patrons scrambled in disarray, running for the exit. Many hit the deck, crawling on their bellies, heading for cover – utter chaos ensued. Captain Henry's Cav Hat was gone.

A TURN OF EVENTS

In a twist of fate, one of the Marine Tomcat pilots was shot down several weeks later and was in grave danger while waiting for rescue. In response to the rescue call, the Smiling Tigers, who were operating nearby, headed to assist the downed Marine pilot. With impressive flying skills, heroic effort, and teamwork with their Marine counterparts, the pilot was rescued and flown to safety.

A week or so later, the Tomcat pilots of VMA-311 arrived unannounced in the Smiling Tigers area with beer, booze, steaks, and a desire to party. The night quickly transformed into an enjoyable gathering filled with good food, laughter, and singing. By the end of the evening, the Tomcats were inducted as honorary members of The Choir. It was a great time for everyone involved.

As the party neared its conclusion, the Tomcat commander stood to express his gratitude to the aviators of The Smiling Tigers. It was at this moment that Captain Henry's Cav Hat was brought out from its hiding place, and the crowd went wild – the

Cav Hat was back! And it acquired a new look: A large red and yellow Tomcat patch was attached to the rear crown.

Mike Henry's Cav Hat
Photo Courtesy of Mike Henry

The Tomcat patch still adorns Mike Henry's hat, serving as a vivid reminder of great times with good friends and fellow brothers in combat!

B TROOP GUNS

B Troop, 2nd of the 17th Air Cavalry was stationed at Camp Eagle and used the callsign Banshee. The aeroweapons platoon, commonly referred to as "Guns," flew the AH-1G Cobra gunship. Their operational area in I Corps typically encompassed the A Shau Valley to the Rockpile, an area notorious for its fierce combat with the North Vietnamese Army in 1971.

The B Troop Guns were highly skilled pilots and demonstrated a strong sense of pride and camaraderie. In addition to their cavalry hats, the Guns wore long red and white scarves patterned after the troop guidon and emblazoned with "B Troop, 2nd of 17th Cavalry" across the colors. These bold and prideful cavalry troopers donned their cavalry hats and colorful scarves when frequently visiting the Division Artillery (Div Arty) Club, where they enjoyed the opportunity to playfully tease and annoy the artillery gunners.

The following photo of B Troop Guns was taken at the request of Captain Eric "Beetle" Bailey, a short-timer who was nearing his DEROS date and would soon depart Vietnam. Beetle wanted to capture the moment he flew with the "Guns."

In the photo, Beetle is third from the right. Featured in the following story is Warrant Officer Gary Ryan, second from the left, and Warrant Officer Robert Hume, first on the left.

B Troop Guns – 2nd of the 17th Air Cavalry
Photo Courtesy of Gary Ryan

A BAD DAY FOR THE BANSHEES

On February 10, 1971, twenty-year-old Warrant Officer Gary Ryan, known by his callsign Banshee 24, was piloting a Cobra gunship on a hunter-killer mission in the Hamburger Hill area of I Corps. This region was notorious for its heavy concentration of North Vietnamese Army forces, making it a highly dangerous area for any air operations.

Flying at an altitude of three hundred feet, Ryan positions his gunship above and behind his scout pilot and close friend, Warrant Officer Mark Robertson, who goes by the callsign Red Oak 17. Robertson, who is flying at treetop level, follows a well-used trail in the valley between two hills covered in dense jungle.

As Ryan watches the small scout helicopter gracefully weave left and right along the trail, he hears Robertson call on the radio, "Banshee 24, Red Oak 17, it looks like a lot of people have been moving along this trail in the past twenty-four hours." Ryan replies, "Roger that."

RED OAK 17 IS GONE!

Suddenly, a chilling *whump, whump, whump* sound pierces the air, and Ryan's heart drops as he watches in horror while Mark's helicopter tumbles through the air, crashes to the ground, and erupts into a catastrophic fireball.

Instinctively, Gary dives toward the crash site, fully aware that there is nothing he can do to save his friend. As he glances to the right, he notices what initially appear to be ants but are actually enemy soldiers scrambling through the open areas on the hillside. To his shock, Gary then sees large .51-caliber tracer rounds passing below his Cobra. He quickly pulls in power and climbs out of the valley just as the enemy gunfire ceases.

After climbing to altitude, Gary calls troop headquarters to report the loss of Mark Robertson and his gunner, Sergeant Joseph Pietrzak. He also provides the grid coordinates of the enemy location and the approximate location of the crash site.

As Gary flies back to Camp Eagle, an intense wave of emotion washes over him. He is devastated and haunted by the sight of his dear friend, Mark Robertson, who was tragically lost in the explosive crash. A deep anger simmers within him, fueled by the painful realization that he was powerless to intervene and save his friend. The weight of grief and frustration bears heavily on his heart.

Upon returning to Camp Eagle, Gary descends to a hover above the runway and taxies to the Banshee revetments. There, he gently sets his Cobra gunship down on the PSP metal planking and shuts down the turbine engine. As the rotor blades slow to a stop, Gary removes his flight helmet, swings the canopy upward, and climbs out.

With overwhelming sadness, Gary slowly walks toward the troop area. After covering about forty feet, he is approached by Warrant Officer Robert Hume, who asks Gary how he is holding up. The following photo was taken at that moment. The profound look of shock and disbelief on this young warrior's face is testimony to the horrors of war endured by countless American soldiers fighting in the Vietnam War.

B Troop Gunship Pilot WO1 Gary Ryan on the Left
WO1 Robert Hume on the Right
Photo Courtesy of Gary Ryan

"My Cav Hat Decided to Fly"

In late 1971, after enduring a series of monotonous non-flying assignments at Fort Rucker, Alabama, Chief Warrant Officer 2 Bob Monette volunteered to return to Vietnam. His request was promptly approved.

Prior to his departure, Monette attended the Cobra gunship transition course and the Instructor Pilots (IP) course. Bob mused at the time, "Thinking the war was winding down, I imagined that flying a Cobra gunship in air-conditioned comfort through the friendly skies of Southeast Asia would be an absolute dream job. Boy, was I in for a surprise – hello, 1972 Easter Offensive!"

Bob Monette arrived in South Vietnam for his second tour in mid-March 1972. Monette was assigned to F Troop, 9th Cavalry flying Cobra gunships with the callsign Saber 20. F Troop was based at Bien Hoa Army Airfield, about twenty-four klicks northeast of Saigon in III Corps.

It wasn't long before Bob found himself among the Cav – a proud and daring group of cavalry troopers who bravely took the fight to the enemy, unleashed awesome firepower from above, and partied hard in the evenings. And Monette loved every moment of it, saying, "Amidst Cav Hats, Cav Boots, and out-of-regulation mustaches, I was in Heaven."

"The Perfect Hat for Vietnam"

After several weeks, Bob received his long-awaited Cav Hat. He later commented, "I knew this was for me. The perfect hat for Vietnam. It kept the sun out of your eyes, the rain off your face, you could sleep under it, and most importantly, you could drink out of it."

Monette proudly wears his Cav Hat every day, a symbol of his dedication and honor in serving with the cavalry. But then, several weeks later, the unthinkable happens – Bob loses his cherished hat.

After enduring forty-five grueling days flying up Thunder Road to An Loc, the F Troop Cav team finally earns a well-deserved night and day off. Eager to celebrate, a small group of cavalry troopers pile into a Huey and take off for the "library" in Vung Tau. (Note: "library" was the code word for a night of bar hopping and revelry.)

After a night of carousing in Vung Tau, the troopers return to the airfield to prepare for the flight back to Bien Hoa. Bob climbs into the passenger compartment and takes his seat on the far-left side, near the cargo door. Once settled, he places his beloved Cav Hat under his jump seat. The designated pilot, a cavalry trooper who refrained from the evening's libations, cranks the Huey's turbine engine, and the rotor blades start turning in the still night air. Then, minutes later, he pulls pitch and the helicopter lifts off into the starlit sky of South Vietnam.

THERE SHE GOES...

Flying smoothly at 2,000 feet above ground level (AGL), Bob savors the cool night air, a welcome reprieve from the sweltering, hot, and humid days in South Vietnam. Suddenly, a flash catches his attention as his beloved cavalry hat is swept from under his seat and out the cargo door, disappearing through the glow of the Huey's navigation lights. Monette's treasured cavalry hat is gone.

The following morning, Bob takes to the skies in a Cobra helicopter, flying as part of a hunter/killer team that includes a scout helicopter and another gunship. During the mission, they decide to divert their flight path to the area where Bob had lost his cavalry hat. Monette envisions finding papa-san behind his water buffalo, proudly wearing the black cavalry hat adorned with a Warrant Officer 2 bar. However, as they scour the area, the harsh reality sets in: His cherished cavalry hat is lost forever.

Upon returning to Bien Hoa, Bob orders a new Cav Hat. Weeks later, he receives the hat and wears it with pride for the remainder of his tour.

Bob's Combat Service

Bob Monette served two tours in Vietnam and earned numerous decorations. He received the Silver Star for his actions in 1972 as a Huey aircraft commander, bravely navigating intense enemy fire to rescue the crew of a downed US Air Force C-130 transport aircraft.

In another mission, Monette provided suppressive fire cover for his wingman, who had been shot down by an SA-7 heat-seeking missile. This story appears later in this chapter, titled "Did You Get My Cav Hat?"

During his time as a Cobra pilot, Bob estimated being targeted by fifteen SA-7 missiles and was hit by one; however, he managed to recover safely, earning him the prestigious "Broken Wing" lapel pin.

Present Times

After a distinguished career in the Army, Bob retired in 1991 as a Master Army Aviator with 6,000 accident-free flight hours and 1,600 combat hours. In 2019, CW4 (Ret.) Bob Monette was inducted into the Army Aviation Hall of Fame in recognition of his courageous combat actions as well as his later contributions to the attack warfare community.

Today, Monette continues to honor the 1st Cavalry by wearing his Cav Hat at helicopter pilot reunions and various military gatherings, a testament to his pride in the cavalry and the bonds formed during his service. Bob's distinguished Cav Hat is featured on the cover of this book.

CW2 Bob Monette and Crew Chief SGT John C. Larkin
Photo Courtesy of Bob Monette

"You Shot My Cav Hat!"

In January 1971, Captain Larry Brown was scout platoon leader for Echo Troop, 1st of the 9th Air Cavalry based out of Lai Khe, located forty-two klicks north of Saigon in III Corps. His callsign was El Lobo White.

Larry had recently been promoted to captain, yet there were no insignia available to reflect his new rank. One of the pilots, returning from another military base, obtained what was available: oversized captain bars worn by the Marines. Brown attached these large captain bars high on the crown of his prized Cav Hat.

Larry acquired this hat on his first Vietnam tour in 1967-68. The Stetson was in pristine condition, except for one of the hat cords, which bore the marks of a near miss, having been nicked by shrapnel while flying scouts for B Troop, 1st of the 9th Air Cavalry in 1968.

"Pink Team" Mission

On this day, Larry is flying an OH-6A scout helicopter on a two-aircraft "pink team" hunter-killer mission. His "gun cover" is provided by Captain Paul Dagnon, the gun platoon leader, flying an AH-1G Cobra gunship. His callsign is El Lobo Red. Brown and Dagnon are the two senior pilots in Echo Troop, each having over twenty months in country. As platoon leaders, Larry and Paul have adopted their platoon's identifier as their nicknames: Larry is "White," and Paul is "Red."

The area of operations (AO) for this mission is approximately eight to ten klicks southwest of Lai Khe where a large contingent of the NVA are suspected to be operating

Arriving at the flight line around sunup, Larry does a preflight inspection of the critical aircraft components. At the same time, his crew chief/gunner also inspects the aircraft before readying his M-60 machine gun and ammunition for today's expected contact with the enemy. His observer, also armed with an M-60, arrives a few minutes later.

After completing his preflight inspection, Captain Brown removes his Cav Hat and places it on top of the instrument console, against the Plexiglass windscreen. Then, Larry climbs into the cockpit on the right side, fastens his lap belt/shoulder harness, dons his flight helmet, and prepares to start the turbine engine.

Nearby, Captain Dagnon performs a similar preflight inspection before removing his Cav Hat and placing it on the shelf behind the pilot's seat in the Cobra gunship. Then Paul climbs aboard and readies his aircraft to start the engine.

Soon, both helicopters are at operating rpm, come to a hover, and taxi to the runway apron. Then Larry places a radio call to the Lai Khe airfield tower saying, "Lai Khe tower, this is El Lobo White with a flight of two departing to the south." The tower replies, "White, you are clear to depart runway two three; altimeter two, niner, niner, zero." Brown replies, "Two, niner, niner, zero, Roger that." Then the pink team helicopters hover forward to the center of the runway, do a pedal turn to the left, and slowly gain airspeed as they take off to the southwest.

When Larry arrives at the AO, he reduces his airspeed to between 10 and 15 knots, flying at treetop level while scanning for any signs of enemy activity. At the same time, Paul enters a wide circle around the Loach while flying at 800 feet AGL.

"Taking Fire"

Initially, Brown sees nothing unusual. Then, he comes upon footprints, and suddenly he is under fire from NVA soldiers armed with AK-47 rifles. Larry calls "Taking Fire" as his gunner returns fire with the M-60 machine gun. Brown banks the Loach to the right to move away from the heavily occupied area.

Circling back, Larry makes a high-speed pass over the area while his gunner engages the enemy soldiers with his M-60 machine gun. Then, as they pass over the heaviest concentration of the enemy, the observer drops a smoke grenade to mark the target for the Cobra gunship. At the same time, Paul banks his Cobra toward the smoke, drops the gunship's nose, and enters a steep dive, aligning his aircraft on the target.

"Taking Hits"

Paul executes several gun runs, expending 12-pound rockets, 40mm grenades, and minigun fire into the enemy position, each time receiving small arms fire from the NVA soldiers below. On his third pass, an AK-47 round hits the Plexiglass canopy, passing behind Dagnon's head and hitting his Cav Hat resting on the shelf. Paul calls, "Taking hits," as he feels his hat brush against his right shoulder.

Returning to Lai Khe airfield, the two helicopters hover to the Echo Troop staging area where Larry and Paul shut down their aircraft. As the rotor blades slow to a stop, Paul unbuckles his shoulder harness and steps out of the Cobra's cockpit on the right side. He reaches back into the cockpit to retrieve his Cav Hat and discovers a bullet hole in the crown. And his aircraft has taken five or six hits from enemy small arms fire.

Later that evening, the gun and scout pilots gather together in a gunship trooper's hooch to relax, have a drink, and celebrate another successful day in the skies over South Vietnam. As usual, the friendly banter between the scouts and guns involves a certain amount of "one-upmanship."

"IF IT WAS ANYONE BUT YOU..."

Larry and Paul are best of friends, but that doesn't deter them from being in each other's face with outrageous claims of flying expertise. At one point, Larry, who is wearing his Cav Hat propped back on his head, tells Paul, "Red, if you were a better pilot, your Cav Hat wouldn't have a bullet hole in it." Paul replies, "White, your hat doesn't have a bullet hole. I'll fix that." Then, to everyone's surprise, Paul, who is directly in front of Larry, points his 38-caliber revolver at the top of Larry's hat and fires a shot. The bullet enters Larry's hat precisely between the two large captain's bars and exits the top of the crown.

The room falls eerily quiet as everyone's attention is drawn to Larry's Cav Hat. Brown removes his hat, sticks his finger through the bullet hole, and turns to Paul, saying, "Red, if it was anyone but you, they would be dead now." The room erupts with laughter.

Larry Brown's Cav Hat
Chopstick Showing Path of Bullet
That Nicked the Left-Side Captain Bar
Photo Courtesy of Larry Brown

The Rest of the Story

You might think this is the end of the story. But, no, it continues... Two days later, Larry and Paul are working their pink teams in the same area. At some point, Brown's team returns to Lai Khe to refuel. While sitting on the refueling pad Larry monitors the troop's radio frequency.

Back at the AO, in the other pink team, Paul Dagnon is flying a Cobra gunship while covering his scout helicopter, flown by Warrant Officer Lou Rochat. Lou is following a well-used trail through the jungle when he suddenly comes upon a large contingent of NVA soldiers. Calling, "Taking fire," Lou banks right to evade the enemy.

Hearing Lou's radio call, Paul banks his Cobra, drops the nose, and unleashes rockets and minigun fire into the area just vacated by Rochat. While climbing and circling back for another gun run, Dagnon glances back to see Rochat's Loach lying on its side – Lou is shot down!

Paul continues his turn and lines up for another gun run to provide suppressive fire around the crash site. While passing over the area, Paul looks down to see Lou's door gunner standing near the crashed Loach, firing his M-60 machine gun into the woods.

While awaiting the arrival of another Loach to evacuate Lou and his gunner, Paul makes multiple gun runs unloading salvo after salvo of rockets, grenades, and minigun fire into the enemy stronghold near the downed scout. On the third attack, Paul's Cobra takes multiple hits (later determined to be fourteen) from small arms fire. Paul calls on the troop radio, "Taking hits, taking hits!"

Recovering from the gun run and climbing to the right, Dagnon realizes he is bleeding. Using the intercom, he tells his front-seat pilot, "I'm hit. You've got it." Paul's front seat is "Lobo

6," the troop commander, Major John Retterer, who says, "I've got it," and takes the controls.

After releasing the flight controls, Paul discovers that shrapnel from the enemy bullets hit his upper right arm and shoulder, and something is in his eyes.

Then, he realizes the Master Caution light and Hydraulic systems lights are illuminated. Losing hydraulics is serious. Paul knows he has a limited time before the controls stiffen. Dagnon recovers the flight controls and looks for an open area to land his disabled aircraft. He calls on the radio, "El Lobo Red has lost hydraulics. We are setting down west of the AO."

The Rescue

Having heard Paul's radio call, Larry promptly lifts off and returns to the AO. By the time Brown arrives, Rochat and his gunner have been picked up by another Loach. Dagnon and Lobo 6 have landed, have shut down the crippled aircraft, and are heading west, away from the enemy. Brown goes after them.

As Larry scans the dense underbrush, he finally spots Dagnon and Lobo 6 maneuvering through the thick trees and scrub brush. He lands his Loach in a nearby open area and waits as the two pilots scramble to climb into the rear compartment of his aircraft.

The situation is critical; enemy troops are closing in on their location, and the lives of both pilots depend on a swift evacuation. A wave of concern washes over Larry. His Loach is heavily loaded with ammo, a full load of fuel, and his two crewmembers. He realizes that adding two more passengers – each weighing over 200 pounds – will make it nearly impossible to get the heavy Loach airborne.

With the two gunship pilots onboard, Larry pulls in all the power possible, and the small aircraft can barely get its skids light on the ground. By cautiously moving the cyclic control, Larry slides his Loach forward, bumping off and onto the ground until the small helicopter reaches translational lift and starts to slowly climb. They've made it!

Upon arriving at Lai Khe airfield, Paul is offloaded at the Aid Station. After medical evaluation, Dagnon is loaded into a Huey and flown to 93rd Evacuation Hospital in Long Binh, where he is treated for arm wounds and shrapnel debris in his eyes.

The following day, Larry visits Paul Dagnon in the hospital, telling him, "Red, this would not have happened if you hadn't shot my hat." Paul does his best to laugh, wincing with pain from his injuries.

The following photo was taken during that visit. Note that Paul is "in uniform," wearing his Cav Hat.

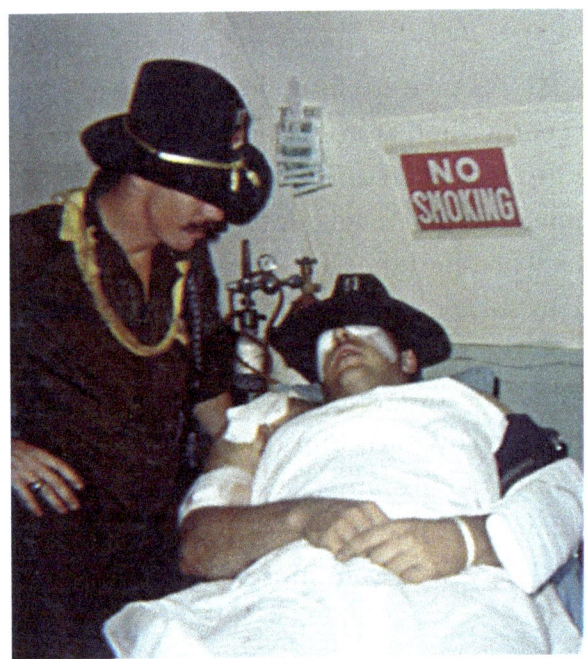

Captain Larry Brown and Captain Paul Dagnon
93rd Evacuation Hospital, Long Binh, 1971
Photo Courtesy of Larry Brown

Sometime later, Dagnon was medevaced to Japan to receive treatment for shrapnel debris that had lodged in his eyes. After a full recovery, Paul, who was nearing his DEROS date, was transferred back to the United States. The two pilots kept in touch but would not see each other again for another twenty years.

Later...

Captain Larry Brown proudly wore his "wounded" cavalry hat with a bullet hole between his captain bars for the remainder of his tour in Vietnam. After thirty years of dedicated service in the Army, Larry retired in 1996 with the rank of colonel. He still keeps his original Cav Hat as a reminder of the camaraderie he shared with his fellow troopers and his immense pride in having served with the air cavalry in Vietnam.

> **Note**: If you take a closer look at Larry's Cav Hat, shown earlier in this story, you'll notice there is a hole in the upper crown and a split in the brim. As Larry explained, "The 'magic spell' on my Cav Hat was broken when Red shot it. Later in my tour, my hat was struck by shrapnel in both the brim and crown."
>
> Also note the two ventilation holes in the crown of Larry's hat. This early Stetson Cav Hat from 1967 has two ventilation grommets on each side of the crown. It's noteworthy that Stetson phased out these vents, making Larry's hat even more unique.

The "Quaker Hat"

In September 1972, Captain Doug Madigan was assigned to F Troop, 9th Cavalry, stationed at Bien Hoa Airbase in III Corps. Upon arriving by jeep, Doug stepped out, grabbed his duffle bag, and was immediately greeted by two anxious Cobra pilots from D Troop, 229th Assault Helicopter Battalion. With an air of urgency, they quickly commandeered the jeep for a trip to Saigon, where they would catch their DEROS flight.

Madigan suddenly realizes that the two pilots were his classmates at West Point. Captain Mike Matthews, one of the pilots, turns to Doug and says, "Hey, would you like to have my Cav Hat?" as he tosses the black hat to Madigan, who instinctively catches it. Doug replies with a hearty "Thank You" as the two captains head off to Saigon. As he walks away, proudly holding the Cav Hat, Doug can't help but think, *What an incredible gift!*

Upon arriving in the F Troop area, it was eerily quiet, and no one was in sight. Then, Madigan discovered the entire troop gathered for a solemn memorial service honoring one of the scout pilots who had been shot down and killed. On the table before them lay the trooper's Cav Hat and boots, powerful symbols of his bravery and ultimate sacrifice. The atmosphere was heavy with grief, serving as a poignant reminder of the devastating realities of war and the profound loss endured by those who fought alongside the courageous scout pilot.

Afterward, Captain John Whitehead, the scout platoon leader, met Doug and showed him to his hooch. After discussing F Troop operations, they examined Madigan's cavalry hat, only to realize it wasn't a Stetson but another brand. Doug tried it on, but it was too small, and the flat-brimmed hat sat perched atop his head. "Oh well," Doug lamented, "it didn't cost me anything."

This unconventional hat with its flat brim set Doug apart from the other F troopers, who all wore standard Cav Hats. This distinctive headgear made Captain Madigan an unmistakable presence at any gathering. Before long, the other troopers began affectionately calling his Cav Hat the "Quaker hat."

"YA GOTTA LOVE THE CAV!"

Years later, Doug bought a Stetson cavalry hat. While attending a Vietnam Helicopter Pilots Association (VHPA) reunion, his fellow F Troop pilots decided to give the hat a proper "breaking in." They filled the crown with beer, bourbon, and various other alcoholic beverages before insisting that Doug drink the unsavory mixture. As Doug later remarked, "Ya gotta love the Cav!"

Doug Madigan's Stetson Cav Hat
2025 VHPA Reunion in St. Louis, MO
Red/White Bullwhip Squadron Pin on Crown

"I Extended My Tour for a Cav Hat"

Chief Warrant Officer 2 Perry Smith served with B Company, 4th Aviation Battalion, also known as the "Black Jacks," from 1969 to 1970. Based in Pleiku, he flew Huey helicopters in the Central Highlands, performing various single-ship missions. These included transporting Long-Range Reconnaissance Patrols (LRRPs) and Republic of Korea (ROK) Special Forces missions and occasionally transporting generals or other dignitaries.

My First Cav Hat Incident

In late 1969, Smith was assigned to pick up Major General Glen Walker, the commanding officer of the 4th Infantry Division. Having flown General Walker to fire bases on several occasions before, Perry was well-acquainted with the mission, making this task seem routine yet significant.

After picking up General Walker and his staff officer at Camp Enari, Perry received instructions to land at Camp Holloway Army Airfield. He was directed to shut down his helicopter and wait for the arrival of a "special guest" for that day's mission. After setting down on the runway apron, General Walker and his staff officer departed the helicopter while Smith and his copilot proceeded to shut down the turbine engine.

After a brief wait, the General's staff officer approached the door of the helicopter and gave a thumbs-up signal, indicating that the general would be there soon. Perry and his copilot immediately began the Huey startup procedure, and soon the rotor blades were spinning smoothly at idle RPM. While they continued with the run-up procedure, Perry paid no attention to who was boarding the aircraft. Once everyone was on board, General Walker used the intercom to inform Perry that they were heading north, toward Kon Tum.

About twenty minutes into the flight, Perry was informed that they would be landing in a large basin just short of Kon Tum. A short while later, Smith spotted the basin, which contained a vast open field. As they approached the field, he noticed rows of tents and a perimeter lined with trucks and armored vehicles, including several tanks.

As Smith closed on the field, he was instructed to land on the western side of the tents, near a particularly large green tent. General Walker then said, "Smitty, the general would like you to hover closer to the large tent." At that moment, Perry realized that there was another general on board – one who held a higher rank than General Walker.

As the helicopter hovered closer, the rotor wash started to lift the tent canvas, and two senior officers rushed out from inside. On the left, an Army colonel, wearing a black cavalry hat, was waving his arms frantically, signaling for Smith to back off. Just then, Perry heard over the intercom, "General Abrams wants to land close to the tent." General Abrams! Smith had no idea he was transporting the MACV commander.

At that moment, the rotor wash lifted the colonel's Cav Hat, sending it soaring into the distance behind him. It landed in the dirt and cartwheeled away. The colonel stopped in his tracks and, with a look of disgust, glared directly at Perry. It became clear that the colonel faced a dilemma: Should he chase after his cherished hat or stay to greet General Abrams? After several moments of contemplation, he decided to run after his hat. The colonel held his cavalry hat in high regard and didn't want to greet the general "uncovered."

A short while later, Smith was instructed to stop hovering forward and set the Huey down. As the skids touched down, Perry looked up to see the colonel emerge from the side of the tent, brushing the dirt off his Cav Hat. He walked toward the

Huey, stopped abruptly, came to attention, and gave General Abrams a sharp salute as he stepped off the helicopter.

After saluting the general, the colonel turned to look at Perry and tipped his hat with a smile on his face. All was forgiven once he realized Smith was only following orders.

MY SECOND CAV HAT INCIDENT

One day, Perry witnessed a Huey helicopter from the 1st of the 9th Cavalry touch down at a Special Forces base. After shutting their aircraft down, the two pilots emerged from the helicopter and proudly donned their black Cav Hats before walking to Operations. The sight was undeniably impressive, leaving Smith thinking, *I really would like to fly with the Cav and wear a Cav Hat someday.*

MY THIRD CAV HAT INCIDENT

Later, Smith rescued a scout pilot from the 1st of the 9th Cavalry who had been shot down about sixteen klicks south of An Khe. The scout pilot carried his Cav Hat with him in the Loach and was wearing it when he climbed aboard Perry's Huey. Once again, Smith was impressed by the 1st of the 9th and their distinctive black cavalry hats.

PERRY EXTENDS HIS TOUR

In August 1970, Smith accepted an offer to extend his deployment for an additional six months. He requested to join the 1st of the 9th Cavalry and was assigned to Charlie Troop, operating out of Phouc Vinh. There, he flew Huey helicopters transporting Blue Teams. The Blue Teams were a small, heavily armed "quick reaction force (QRF)" tasked with reconnoitering suspected enemy positions, assessing battle damage, supporting

Long-Range Reconnaissance Patrols (LRRPs) in contact with the enemy, and securing downed aircraft.

Almost immediately after joining Charlie Troop, Perry ordered his Cav Hat. When it finally arrived several weeks later, he eagerly opened the box labeled "Stetson Hats." As he removed the hat and placed it on his head, a sense of pride washed over him. *Perfect fit*, he thought. With care, he attached his rank insignia and the 1-9 Cavalry crossed sabers to the front of the crown. From that moment on, Perry proudly wore his Cav Hat wherever he went.

Perry shared his feelings about his cavalry hat, saying, "My Cav Hat holds a special place in my heart because it represents the pride I have in serving with the cavalry. It's a symbol of the dedication, respect, loyalty, and amazing camaraderie I share with my fellow cavalry brothers. I truly feel honored and blessed to have served alongside such incredible people!"

The following photo shows Perry Smith's Cav Hat on proud display in his home.

Perry Smith's Cav Hat

"Did You Get My Cav Hat?"

First Lieutenant Bruce McKenty arrived in Vietnam in July 1972 and was assigned to F Troop, 9th Cavalry, operating out of Bien Hoa Airbase. Almost immediately upon his arrival, Bruce was relegated to a detail of officers tasked with finding a new bar for the troop's officers' club.

During this period, many American military units were in the process of withdrawing and redeploying back to the United States. This included the 3rd Brigade of the 1st Cavalry Division, and there was a rumor that they had a beautiful teak wood bar in their officers' club. The group of five officers decided to check it out, so they jumped into the back of a five-ton ammo truck and drove to the other side of the Bien Hoa Airbase, where they promptly "appropriated" the teak bar.

The Stetson

While there, Bruce visited the 3rd Brigade supply office. On the counter, he noticed a new Stetson cavalry hat box. McKenty asked the lieutenant about the box, and the lieutenant explained that it had been delivered a week after he received his orders for early departure. Bruce asked if he wanted to sell the hat, and the lieutenant eagerly agreed.

Bruce was thrilled! He had been in Vietnam for less than a week, and he had already obtained his coveted Cav Hat. Upon opening the box, McKenty discovered a pristine black cavalry hat with no decoration other than officer cords. He promptly attached his rank insignia and the F-9 cavalry crossed sabers to the front of the crown. As Bruce described it, "I was a Cobra pilot, and we were 'hot sh*t,' so my hat needed some really cool pins featuring a cobra snake. I acquired a brass cobra silhouette and a coiled cobra snake to place on the sides of the hat. To top it off, I added an impressive yellow 1st Cavalry patch pin and our 9th Cavalry regimental insignia to the backside of the crown. I was ready to roll! Hooah!"

Hunter/Killer Missions

A few days later, Bruce successfully passed his AH-1G Cobra check ride that included carrying a full load of fuel and armament. Then Bruce flew his first hunter/killer mission with Gun Platoon Leader Captain Jimmy Ford. "Jimmy was a great guy and everyone in the Gun platoon had tremendous respect for him," said Bruce, "He was a skilled gunship pilot, and I learned a lot from Jimmy." McKenty went on to say, "Jimmy always brought his Cav Hat on missions and stored it on the shelf behind his seat. I thought that was cool, so I started bringing mine as well."

On this first mission, the two Cobra helicopters and one OH-6A scout helicopter lifted off from Lai Khe airfield, flying 80 knots and about fifty feet above the trees. Upon reaching the area of operations (AO), the two Cobras entered a wide circle around the scout helicopter, each gunship 180 degrees out from each other and flying at about 150 knots, while still on top of the trees. The Cobras were ready to strike if the scout helicopter came under hostile fire.

Bruce asked Jimmy why they were flying at treetop level, and Ford explained the tactics. He recounted how they had lost several Cobras to SA-7 heat-seeking missiles at An Loc during the early days of the Easter Offensive. The missiles targeted the heat signature from the Cobra's exhaust, resulting in explosions that severed the Cobra's tail boom. In each crash, both crewmembers were killed. Jimmy then pointed out, "We are flying in the same area today, and the enemy still has a lot of SA-7 missiles." Little did Bruce know that he would be shot down by an SA-7 missile about five months later in this same area.

During this period, the Army equipped the Huey and Cobra helicopters with exhaust deflectors. This unusual device, which some likened to a toilet bowl, was attached to the engine exhaust where its curved design directed the hot exhaust upward, into the rotor blades. The deflectors proved to be an effective deterrent, and once all F Troop Cobras had the deflectors installed, their tactics evolved. The pilots began flying the Cobras at higher altitudes, which allowed them to observe the scouts more effectively and dive to fire rockets with greater precision.

Hit by an SA-7 Heat-Seeking Missile

On December 3, 1972, Bruce is flying in the front seat/gunner position of an AH-1G Cobra gunship during a hunter/killer mission. The aircraft commander, Chief Warrant Officer 2 Bobby Rinehart, is in the rear, pilot's seat. Their AO is in the Razorback Mountains, southwest of An Loc, and approximately two to three klicks from the Cambodian border. The two Cobras have been on station for about fifteen minutes, flying in wide circles, 180 degrees apart from each other, while covering the scout helicopter below.

Suddenly, Bruce and Bobby hear a loud BOOM, and the Cobra shakes violently from the impact. Then, an eerie silence falls; there's no radio chatter, no intercom, and no sound from the turbine engine – just total silence. It quickly becomes clear that they have lost the engine, hydraulics, and electrical systems.

Bobby immediately enters autorotation, taking the pitch out of the rotor system as the Cobra descends at a forward airspeed of 120 knots. Looking ahead, Bobby notices a series of bomb craters left by a B-52 Arc Light bombing strike. He turns the aircraft toward the craters and pulls back hard on the cyclic control to slow the rapidly descending helicopter.

Smoke and noxious fumes fill the cockpit, making it difficult for Bruce and Bobby to breathe. Yelling loudly to Bobby, Bruce says, "I'm opening the canopy," fully aware that it will be torn off at such high speeds. As the canopy opens, air rushes in, causing the fire to engulf the entire cockpit, particularly around Bobby, who screams in pain. In response, Bobby opens his canopy. With both canopies missing, a powerful crosswind is created, which redirects the fire out the right rear opening.

With the fire threat seemingly behind them, Bobby yells at Bruce to take the controls and help him slow down the disabled aircraft as it continues its descent. Lacking hydraulic power, it takes every ounce of energy for both pilots to gradually reduce the airspeed to 100 knots, then 90 knots, and finally to 80 knots. At that moment, Bruce notices the ground approaching rapidly. He braces himself for impact and loses consciousness.

Chief Warrant Officer 2 Bob Monette, flying the other Cobra gunship, described what he observed: "After an unanswered radio call, I looked to my left and saw my wingman engulfed in flames and descending to the ground. I immediately banked my Cobra to follow him. The disabled gunship hit the ground hard, going at least 50 knots. The main rotor severed the tail boom just as the fuselage bounced upward and rolled inverted, finally coming to rest in a bomb crater."

THE RESCUE

Surviving the impact, Bobby quickly unbuckles his lap belt/shoulder harness and crawls out of the wreckage. Fearing an explosion due to the combination of fire, fuel, and munitions, he starts running but then thinks of Bruce and looks back to see if he made it out. Turning around, he sees McKenty hanging upside down inside what is left of the cockpit, his face covered in blood.

Bobby, unsure whether Bruce is dead or alive, rushes back to the wreckage. Using his knife, he cuts the lap belt, and Bruce falls downward. The impact causes Bruce to awaken slightly. Realizing that McKenty is alive, Bobby pulls him out of the mangled fuselage and carries him to a safe distance from the crash site.

At this point, Bruce is gradually regaining consciousness. The two injured pilots hear a Huey helicopter in the distance but cannot see it due to the thick vegetation surrounding them. They carefully navigate toward the unmistakable sound of the Huey's rotor blades, and soon they come upon an incredible sight: A Huey is sitting in a jungle clearing, ready to rescue them.

In a crippled run, the two approach the Huey piloted by Major George Hewlett, the troop commander. As they reach the open cargo door, the crew chief pulls them into the cargo bay.

Once they are settled in the jump seats, Bruce turns to Bobby and asks, "Did you get my Cav Hat out of the battery compartment?" Bobby looks at Bruce with a look of bewilderment. Then, the two embrace, laughing and crying as they realize they have survived a deadly crash.

Note: In the shock and confusion of the crash, Bruce failed to remember that he didn't wear his Cav Hat to the flight line that morning. Bobby, however, knew there was no Cav Hat in the aircraft.

The Huey helicopter lifts off, transporting the two survivors to Lai Khe, where they are transferred to another Huey. They are then flown to the 3rd Field Hospital in Saigon, where they receive treatment for their injuries.

Both pilots sustained burns, but Bobby's burns were significantly more severe than Bruce's. While one medical team cleaned and bandaged Bobby's burns, another team treated Bruce's lacerations on his head, face, and upper body. Afterward, the two pilots were released and returned to their home base at Bien Hoa. Much later, Bruce learned he had suffered a skull fracture and three fractured vertebrae.

Present Day

After serving in Vietnam, Bruce McKenty enjoyed a distinguished twenty-year career in the Army, where he held various command and staff positions in Army Aviation and Field Artillery. He retired in 1991 with the rank of lieutenant colonel. Bruce remarked, "My Cav Hat is a significant and important symbol of my life. I still have it and wear it on important occasions, such as reunions and vacation trips with my fellow F-Troopers."

> The following photo shows Bruce wearing his Cav Hat after his Cobra was struck by a 51-caliber armor-piercing round fired from an NVA anti-aircraft machine gun in August 1972. The bullet entered the left side of Bruce's armor-plated seat, tore through the pocket of his flight suit pants, and left fragments of the armor-plated ceramic tile embedded in his left buttock. The bullet then ricocheted off the back of the armored seat and lodged in the right side of the seat. Bruce still keeps the bullet as a reminder of his close call in combat.

First Lieutenant Bruce McKenty
Holding 51-cal. Bullet Next to Entry Hole in Cobra
Photos courtesy of Bruce McKenty

F Troop Guns
(l to r) CPT Jimmy Ford, 1LT Bruce McKenty,
and CW2 Bob Monette

(l to r) Bob Monette, Doug Madigan, and Bruce McKenty
F-9 Cavalry Troopers at the 2025 VHPA Reunion in St. Louis, MO

THE HIPPIE HAT BAND AND THE PEACOCK

Some cavalry troopers added creative touches to their cavalry hats. One of the more noticeable decorations was the addition of colorful hat bands. Warrant Officer John Shafer, a scout pilot for B Troop, 7th Squadron of the 17th Air Cavalry, wore a red, white, and blue "hippie hat band" on his cavalry hat. This colorful hat band was given to John by Warrant Officer Garland Hines, another scout pilot, who had received two hat bands from his wife.

One day, John was walking to the flight line when he came across a dead peacock that had been struck by a jeep. John plucked a feather from the peacock and stuck it in his hat. Soon after, all the scout pilots proudly wore feathers in their Cav Hats.

The commanding officer, Major Glenn Carr, was not fond of the feathers, but for the sake of morale, he allowed the scouts to continue wearing them. Years later, retired Lieutenant Colonel Carr recalled, "I seem to remember a warrant officer shot the peacock," as he laughed and pointed at Shafer.

Warrant Officer John Shafer
Scout Pilot, B Troop 7-17 Cav
Courtesy of John Shafer

John Shafer
2024 Veterans Day Parade, Auburn, WA
Courtesy of John Shafer

"The VC Shot My Cav Hat and Hit My Coffee"

In the summer of 1971, First Lieutenant Joe Eszes was the Aero Scout platoon leader with C Troop, 16th Air Cavalry, based out of Can Tho Army Airfield in IV Corps, essentially the Mekong Delta. The troop's callsign and nickname was Darkhorse.

Joe, who began his military career by enlisting in the Marines, had transferred to the Army, attended Army flight school as a warrant officer, and received a battlefield commission as a regular Army officer. Joe was an experienced OH-6A helicopter pilot and relished the thrill, excitement, and challenges that came with flying low-level scout missions in Vietnam.

Arriving at the flight line around sunrise, Joe carefully placed his prized Stetson, a stainless-steel Thermos full of hot coffee, and his CAR-15 rifle in the left front seat of the Loach, where he used the lap belt and shoulder harness to secure the items for flight. Then, Eszes and his door gunner began their preflight inspection of the aircraft and its onboard munitions.

The Darkhorse OH-6A helicopters were configured identically. The pilot operated from the right seat, while the gunner rode in the right side of the rear compartment, positioned to fire out the right-side door. An XM-134 minigun was mounted on the left pylon, equipped with 2,500 rounds of ammunition stored in a long container on the floor of the rear compartment. The door gunner fired a handheld M-60 machine gun and carried an additional 3,000 rounds of 7.62mm link ammunition. The crew also transported approximately 100 to 120 pounds of improvised C4 explosives/concussion grenade bombs, which were used to destroy bunkers and fighting positions. In addition to all this, they carried a standard load of smoke grenades and trip flares for igniting and burning structures.

THE MISSION

On this day, Darkhorse was flying a "search and destroy" mission consisting of two scouts down, two Cobras gunships high, and a command-and-control Huey. They were supporting the 9th ARVN (Army of the Republic of Vietnam) Division and working in the area near Phung Hiep, approximately thirty-two klicks south of Can Tho and thirty-three klicks northwest of Soc Trang. The weather was clear with no clouds in the skies, and the temperature was in the nineties.

The Phung Hiep area was "bad news." The primary threat came from the Viet Cong's "Soc Trang" Battalion, notorious for their aggressive, ruthless tactics. Previous missions in that area resulted in vicious firefights with the Viet Cong laying down coordinated volleys of small arms fire.

Joe describes what happened: "We let down directly over the village of Phung Hiep and a major four-way canal intersection. Then, we headed west at an altitude of ten to fifteen feet and a ground speed slightly above translational lift, about 10 knots. Within moments after arriving at the area, we came upon newly constructed bunkers and fortified fighting positions. I initiated our standard right-hand turn with the trail Loach in echelon left formation, covering my aircraft. My door gunner commenced firing his machine gun, and immediately, the crap hit the fan with small arms return fire from machine guns and AK-47s."

"TAKING HITS!"

Joe called on the radio, "Breaking right, taking fire, taking hits!" While in a turn, bullets seared through the right-side front door opening. The Plexiglas windscreen and instrument panel sustained bullet damage, as did the floor and the bottom of

Eszes's seat. "The aircraft was still flying and exhibited nothing unusual other than a main rotor vibration," said Joe. "We broke station and headed to the nearest secure area, landed, and did a visual inspection of the bullet damage."

That's when Eszes realized that bullets had struck the left seat, hitting Joe's Thermos in a glancing blow and leaving a small crease along the side of the durable container. And, to his dismay, his cherished Cav Hat took three hits, two through the brim and one through the top of the crown. "I never wore that Stetson again," said Joe. He ordered a new Cav Hat and wore it for the remainder of his tour of duty. Then, just before DEROSing, Joe gave his bullet-ridden cavalry hat to a "wannabe" scout pilot.

AFTER VIETNAM

Joe's next assignment took him to Fort Knox, Kentucky. While there, he met Captain Jim Adamson, who was attending the Air Cavalry Course before his deployment to Vietnam. The two cavalry officers quickly forged a strong friendship, bonding over their shared experiences and aspirations. Before Jim left for Vietnam, Joe kindly presented him with his "indestructible" creased Thermos and flight helmet.

Due to their friendship, Captain Jim Adamson requested and was assigned to Joe's unit, C Troop, 16th Cavalry, where he flew the OH-6A helicopter with the Outcast Scout Platoon. His remarkable journey continued after Vietnam as he became an astronaut, participating in two groundbreaking space shuttle missions: Columbia in 1989 and Atlantis in 1991.

In recognition of his outstanding contributions, Colonel James C. Adamson (Ret.) was inducted into the Army Aviation Hall of Fame in 2007. When asked about the Thermos, Jim remarked, "I held onto that rugged, old Thermos for many years. Unfortunately, it slipped away during several moves, and I can no longer find it today."

ARMY CAREER AND CAV HAT

Joe Eszes had a remarkable and distinguished career in the U.S. Army. Throughout his service as an air cavalry troop commander, an air cavalry squadron commander, and an air cavalry brigade commander, he proudly wore his second Cav Hat. Now displayed prominently in his home, this iconic hat stands as a powerful symbol of his dedication and bravery during the Vietnam War, serving as a constant reminder of his proud service in the air cavalry.

> **Note**: In December 1971, Joe Eszes was nominated for the Medal of Honor. This nomination ultimately led to him receiving the Distinguished Service Cross in 1974 for his heroic actions as a Huey pilot when Joe made multiple attempts, under extreme enemy fire, to rescue the crew of two downed scout helicopters. The award citation reads, in part, "Five times First Lieutenant Joe Eszes braved death in an attempt to rescue his fallen comrades."
>
> In 2017, Colonel Joseph W. Eszes (Ret.) was inducted into the Army Aviation Hall of Fame. He is a Master Army Aviator with 3,100 hours, 1,671 hours in combat.

COL (Ret) Joe Eszes's Cav Hat
Photo Courtesy of Joe Eszes

Joe's Original Stetson Hat Box, Circa 1971
Photo Courtesy of Joe Eszes

Silverbelly Cav Hats – Lighthorse Air Cavalry

D Troop, 3rd of the 5th Air Cavalry, proudly known as "Lighthorse," was the first and only cavalry troop to wear the distinctive silverbelly Stetson cavalry hats during the Vietnam War. This unique tradition began in July 1968 when First Lieutenant Ace Cozzalio and two fellow cavalrymen contacted Stetson, requesting they make silverbelly Stetsons for their troop. Stetson agreed and it wasn't long before most Lighthorse pilots were wearing the lighter-color Cav Hats.

When someone inquired about the unique color, Cozzalio promptly explained, "The 5th U.S. Cavalry fought in the Indian Campaigns in the late 1800s. Back then, the lighter-colored cavalry hat was used as the working hat for the horse cavalry, while the black hat served as the dress hat."

While Ace was correct in stating that the lighter-color hat was indeed the working hat for the horse cavalry, no evidence could be found to support the claim that the black hat functioned as a dress hat after the introduction of the "drab"-color 1883 campaign hat. Nevertheless, it's plausible that some cavalry troopers chose to retain their 1876 black hats for formal occasions.

Over the next four years, Lighthorse troopers proudly wore their distinctive silverbelly cavalry hats throughout all daily activities at the Army airfield. And the iconic hats accompanied them in the skies as they flew helicopters on missions.

Whether gathering for roll call or enjoying time at the officers' club, their unique hats unmistakably identified them as proud Lighthorse Air Cavalry troopers.

WO1 Bob Berry and WO1 Ken Lake
Lighthorse Cav Hats

1LT Ace Cozzalio
Lighthorse Air Cavalry

WO1 Steven Sparks
Courtesy of Steven Sparks

The Author's Cav Hat

LIGHTHORSE REFLAGGED

On February 1, 1971, Lighthorse was reflagged from D Troop, 3rd of the 5th Air Cavalry to its new designation as C Troop, 3rd of the 17th Air Cavalry. The troop guidon and Lighthorse insignia were updated to reflect the new troop letter and squadron number designations, while the troop personnel, aircraft, and equipment remained unchanged. Most importantly, Lighthorse troopers continued to wear their iconic silverbelly cavalry hats.

PRESENT DAY

Lighthorse Air Cavalry has held an annual reunion since July 1993. The 2025 reunion took place in Savannah, Georgia, at Hunter Army Airfield. This event was a joint "Cavalry Meet" with C Troop, 3rd of the 17th Air Cavalry, the troop's successor unit.

Today, C Troop has the nickname "Crazyhorse," while the 3rd of the 17th Air Cavalry Squadron has adopted the name "Lighthorse Squadron." (See Chapter 8 for additional information about Lighthorse Squadron.)

In a remarkable display of camaraderie and leadership, Crazyhorse Commander Captain Genevieve McCormick set aside her black Stetson to wear a silverbelly Cav Hat for the event. The photo on the following page captures a joyful moment as Captain McCormick and J. D. Bottorff, Warwagon scout gunner, share a laugh with reunion attendees.

Captain Genevieve McCormick and J. D. Bottorff
Lighthorse/Crazyhorse Cavalry Meet, April 25, 2025

"BILLY JACK" CAV HATS

B Troop, 2nd of the 17th Air Cavalry was activated at Fort Hood, Texas, in late 1968 and deployed to South Vietnam in March 1969. The troop's callsign and nickname was "Banshee."

Several Banshee troopers adorned their Cav Hats with colorful Indian beaded hatbands and feathers. Some even chose to extend the crowns of their hats in the "Billy Jack" style, inspired by the 1967 movie *The Born Losers*, in which the main character, Billy Jack, wore a black, flat-brimmed hat with an open crown and an Indian beaded hatband.

Staff Sergeant Lucious Patterson, shown in the following photo wears his Cav Hat Billy Jack style. Patterson, who deployed to South Vietnam with the troop, was team leader for the scout observers and often flew as the observer/gunner in the Loach. Patterson earned widespread respect for his exceptional marksmanship while firing from a fast-moving scout helicopter.

Staff Sergeant Lucious Patterson
Photo Courtesy of Dan Hilliard

"Did I Just Give My Cav Hat to a Navy Nurse?"

First Lieutenant Steve Pullen, callsign Banshee 11, was a scout pilot with B Troop, 2nd of the 17th Air Cavalry, based out of Camp Eagle. In January 1971, Steve was wounded and medevaced to the Navy hospital ship USS *Sanctuary*, which was stationed offshore. Pullen spent two weeks on the ship recuperating, during which time he met and became friends with a Navy nurse.

After returning to B Troop, Pullen was assigned to conduct maintenance test flights on the OH-6A helicopter. Seizing a unique opportunity, Steve decided to fly to the hospital ship and invite his nurse friend for a short flight. The nurse enjoyed this little adventure, and it soon became a regular occurrence.

During one of those flights, the nurse suggested organizing a flight for her fellow nurses, who would appreciate getting off the ship for a few hours. Pullen suggested that the ideal time for this event would be during a "Cav Night," which takes place on Friday nights at B Troop's club. This gathering is a popular occasion, drawing pilots and officers from B Troop, HQ Troop, and L Company, 75th Rangers. The nurse thought this was ideal, and a date was set.

The "Cav Night"

On the agreed-upon Friday evening, a pilot from B Troop flew a Huey helicopter to the ship where he picked up seven nurses and transported them to Camp Eagle. That night, the club came alive as an incredible band took the stage, and everyone reveled in an unforgettable evening before the nurses were flown back to their ship in the early morning hours. This "special" Cav Night unfolded on several more occasions before Pullen's departure from Vietnam in May 1971.

"I LIKE YOUR HAT," SAID THE NURSE.

During his last Cav Night, the nurse told Steve that she liked his cavalry hat. Since Pullen was preparing to depart Vietnam, he saw this as an opportunity to connect with her, something akin to going steady. In a fleeting moment of infatuation, Steve handed his cherished cavalry hat to the nurse, completely captivated by her charm.

Today, Steve reflects with a sense of loss, saying, "I never saw the nurse again, and I'm left to forever wonder what became of my Cav Hat."

1LT Steve Pullen in Loach on USS *Sanctuary* Helipad
Photo Courtesy of Steve Pullen

ILT Steve Pullen at B Troop "Cav Night"
Photo Courtesy of Steve Pullen

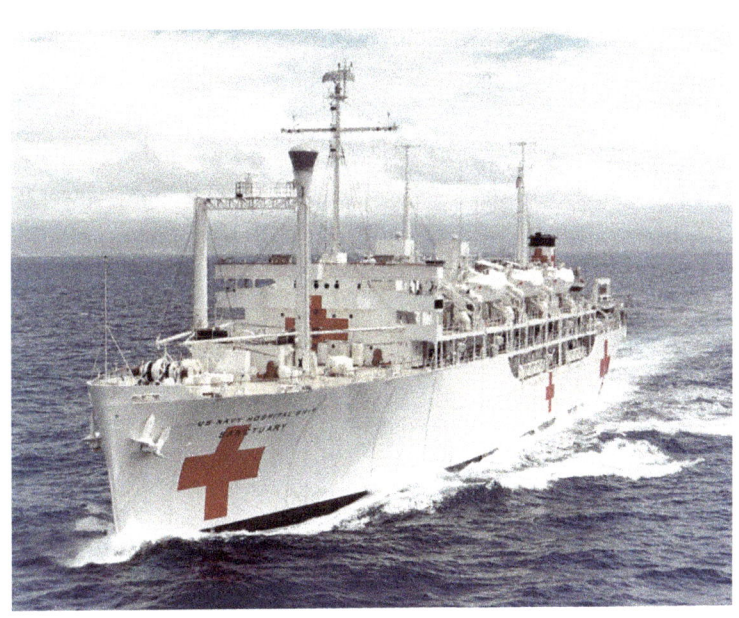

USS *Sanctuary*
Hospital Ship Stationed Offshore South Vietnam
Public Domain Image

"Hell No, I'm Not Removing My Cav Hat!"

In early 1969, after successfully completing the Basic Helicopter Maintenance and Door Gunner School at Fort Rucker, Alabama, Private First Class George Abernathy was assigned to Ansbach, Germany, where he eventually assumed the role of aviation company armorer and was promoted to Specialist 4th Class.

Driven by a desire for greater adventure and excitement, Abernathy was determined to serve as a door gunner in combat. He sought advice from several pilots and crewmembers with firsthand experience in Vietnam. After considering their recommendations, George submitted a request to fly with the scouts of Apache Troop, 1st of the 9th Air Cavalry, 1st Cavalry Division in Vietnam.

Abernathy arrived in Vietnam in December 1969 and was assigned to a desk in flight operations for the 765th Transportation Battalion at Vung Tau. Shortly after his arrival, he submitted another request to join Apache Troop.

Apache Scouts and George's Cav Hat

In June 1971, George's request was granted, and he transferred to Tay Ninh, where he joined the Apache Troop Scouts. After flying a couple of hunter-killer missions as an "oscar," George acquired his coveted Stetson. To Abernathy, wearing this resplendent hat was a distinct honor. He commented, "To me and other troopers, wearing the cavalry hat was like wearing a badge of honor, something you earned at the precarious price of flying scouts."

After gaining considerable experience as an oscar, George took on the responsibility of a "torque" (crew chief/door gunner) and was promoted to Specialist 5. Soon after, Apache Troop relocated to Firebase Buttons at Song Be.

During Abernathy's time with Apache Troop, from June 1970 to February 1971, he flew an impressive 625 combat hours, while facing numerous intense and harrowing experiences. However, the flight he recalls most vividly is his last mission on the day before his DEROS date. On that day, George was flying as the torque for Apache Troop Commander Captain Charles McMenamy on a two-aircraft hunter-killer mission seven to eight klicks into Cambodia.

NVA Regiment Camp

After descending from 3,000 feet altitude to treetop level flight, McMenamy and Abernathy suddenly came upon a large group of substantial structures. It quickly became evident that they had discovered a significant North Vietnamese Army unit, which was later determined to be regimental in size. As they circled the large encampment, it was eerily quiet – they were not being fired upon.

The encampment bore the unmistakable signs of recent use, yet it was hauntingly empty, with no occupants in sight. At one point, McMenamy instructed Abernathy to recon by fire. After expending over 200 rounds of ammunition, there was still no return fire.

It was then that Abernathy saw several chickens grazing near some hooches. He fired into the birds, sending feathers flying everywhere. That got their attention! Suddenly, enemy soldiers emerged from their hiding spots and unleashed a barrage of gunfire at the Loach. AK-74 assault rifles were fired from all directions, with green tracer rounds zipping past the small helicopter.

"TAKING FIRE! TAKING FIRE!"

Upon hearing George yell, "Taking fire! Taking fire, Get the fu** out of here!," McMenamy pulled in power to promptly exit the area while the oscar tossed a smoke grenade to mark the location for the Cobra flying overhead.

Typically, once they flew out of the kill zone, the enemy fire would diminish. But not this time. The enemy's presence was overwhelming, and the AK-47 gunfire was relentless. Clearly, this situation demanded a significantly larger force, including artillery and Air Force bombers.

McMenamy keyed the mike and announced he was getting out of the area and would be climbing to altitude. After ascending to about one hundred feet, with Abernathy firing at any targets of opportunity, they came under heavy .51-caliber anti-aircraft fire, with large tracer rounds slicing dangerously beneath and in front of the rapidly departing Loach.

It wasn't long before they started receiving fire from the second .51-caliber anti-aircraft gun. George commented, "I couldn't count the number of muzzle flashes and tracers, so I started concentrating my efforts towards an individual .51-caliber gun emplacement until it went quiet."

After reaching an altitude of 1,000 feet, the small arms fire ceased, but three .51-caliber machine guns and a light machine gun continued to target the small helicopter. This gunfire persisted as they climbed through 2,000 feet, at which point the light machine gun ceased firing. Shortly after reaching 4,200 feet, all three .51-caliber machine guns stopped firing.

POSTFLIGHT

Upon returning to Firebase Buttons at around 3:00 p.m., McMenamy shut down the Loach. Abernathy did a quick postflight inspection since he needed to prepare for his departure the following morning. During the inspection, George discovered that his aircraft had sustained several hits. He had also fired over 2,500 rounds of 7.62mm ammunition, which led to the destruction of one of the M-60 machine gun barrels due to the extreme heat of continuous gunfire.

"Don't Let Anyone Tell You…"

The following morning, Abernathy sought out Captain McMenamy to shake his hand and thank him for his piloting skills, which had enabled them to escape a precarious situation the day before. As George turned to leave, he paused and looked back at the captain, asking, "Am I allowed to wear my Cav Hat until I am discharged?" McMenamy replied, "Don't let anyone tell you that you have to take it off." George smiled broadly as he continued toward the flight line for his return trip to the States.

On the return flight, the plane made a stop in Japan for refueling, and the soldiers were allowed to disembark at the airport terminal for a break. While there, a Military Police (MP) first lieutenant stopped George and told him that he was out of uniform and must remove his cavalry hat. George responded, "Hell no, I am not removing my cavalry hat. I've earned the right to wear it and won't take it off."

The Military Police officer threatened to arrest Abernathy and detain him in Japan, which would delay his discharge. George responded, "You can call my troop commander, Captain McMenamy, and if that isn't sufficient, you can contact Lieutenant Colonel Carl Putnam, the 1st of the 9th Cavalry Commanding Officer. And if that isn't enough, you can contact the 1st Cavalry Division commanding officer, General George Putnam. All will confirm my right to wear this hat." The lieutenant stood in stunned silence as Abernathy turned and walked away, heading back to the boarding area.

Upon his arrival in Oakland, California, George was discharged from the Army. He then boarded a commercial flight for Seattle, Washington. As he entered the terminal, his brother was there, waiting with a big hug and a welcome home.

Sometime later, George lost his prized Cav Hat and ordered another Stetson. Today, George Abernathy's Cav Hat is proudly displayed in his home office, serving as a testament to his courageous service as a door gunner for the Apache scouts. He wears his Cav Hat during Apache Troop reunions and other military events.

SP4 George Abernathy
Song Be, South Vietnam, July 1970
Photo Courtesy of George Abernathy

George's Cav Hat Today
Photo Courtesy of George Abernathy

My "Gabby Hayes" Cav Hat

In 1969, Captain Robert Frank returned to the United States after completing his first tour in Vietnam as an infantry officer. He was assigned to Fort Polk, Louisiana, which left him feeling more than disappointed, as he believed he deserved a better reward for a year spent dodging bullets in Vietnam.

Captain Frank asked the assignment officer, "Is there anywhere on this planet you can send me besides Fort Polk?" The officer responded, "I see you did quite well on the flight aptitude test. Would you be interested in attending helicopter flight school?" Curious, Robert inquired about the duration of Army flight school, to which the officer replied, "It lasts about ten months." With enthusiasm, Frank said, "Yes, sign me up!" This decision was easy since Robert had previously learned that, as an infantry captain, he would be returning to Vietnam in ten to fourteen months.

Vietnam

After graduating from the U.S. Army Flight School, Captain Frank received orders to Vietnam. He arrived in June 1971 and was assigned to the 1st Cavalry Division based at Bien Hoa Airbase. At that time, the division was in the process of redeploying back to Fort Hood, Texas, except for B Troop, 1st of the 9th Cavalry, which was remaining in Vietnam.

This situation was short-lived, since the B Troop designation was needed at Fort Hood. Consequently, B Troop was redesignated as H Troop, 16th Cavalry, and later became F Troop, 9th Air Cavalry, returning once again to its original regiment, the 9th Cavalry.

F TROOP

In F Troop, Robert was given the callsign Saber 32 and assigned as the blue (Lift) platoon leader, flying Hueys loaded with infantry troops for crew rescue and various ground missions. This role was well-suited to Captain Frank, an infantry officer with previous Vietnam experience as a recon platoon leader.

When Frank reported to the 1st Cavalry, he was told he needed to order a Cav Hat, so he ordered a size seven. When the hat arrived, Robert found it too small, so he decided to wear it forward on his head. However, the wide brim obstructed his vision, so he folded the front brim upward. This worked, but it looked a bit goofy, so he folded the back brim upward to match.

THE SIDEKICK?

Robert took pride in his handiwork and believed his hat had a unique and striking character. However, the "old-timers" gave him a good-natured ribbing, with some saying he resembled Gabby Hayes, the character actor known as a sidekick to John Wayne, Roy Rogers, and Hopalong Cassidy. Robert accepted the teasing with good humor, and over time, he became widely recognized for his distinctive cavalry hat.

Today, Robert's "Gabby Hayes" Cav Hat is proudly displayed in his office bookcase, still covered in dust and dirt from Vietnam that was never brushed from his cherished hat.

Captain Robert Frank
F Troop, 9th Air Cavalry, 1971
Courtesy of Robert Frank

Captain Robert Frank
F Troop, 9th Air Cavalry, 1971
Courtesy of Robert Frank

"Where's Your Cav Hat?"

In February 1972, First Lieutenant Steve Suiter was flying scouts for the Centaurs, F Troop, 4th Air Cavalry. His callsign was Centaur 15. On this day, Suiter was flying a reconnaissance mission in the "Mushroom" area near the Cambodian border.

Steve was flying about twenty-five feet above the ground and following a trail when enemy small arms fire erupts from multiple locations. Suiter utters the renowned air cavalry distress call, "Oh sh*t," and immediately pulls in power as his airspeed increases from 20 to 100 knots. Then he hears the all-too-familiar pinging sound as bullets rip through the thin skin of his aircraft. Suddenly, his Loach noses into the ground, rolling three and one-half times before coming to an abrupt halt with the mangled aircraft resting upside down.

Steve, now precariously hanging in the upper portion of the cockpit, unbuckles his safety harness and falls downward, rolling out of the shattered plexiglass bubble that is partially embedded in the dirt. After standing up and regaining his composure, Suiter sees the Centaur command and control Huey approach to a hover and set down about sixty meters away.

Taking Fire at the Crash Site

First Lieutenant Roger Blaha, aircraft commander of the Huey, recalls, "As I set my Huey down near Steve's crash, I see multiple muzzle flashes in the woods and dirt kicked up from the bullets hitting the ground around the crash site. Steve stands and appears to be momentarily dazed as my crew motions for him to hurry to our aircraft." Meanwhile, the Loach's gunner and observer sprint toward the waiting Huey and promptly climb aboard.

THAT CRAZY SCOUT PILOT

Once the reality of the situation sinks in, Suiter runs toward the rescue aircraft. As he reaches up to grab the cargo door frame, Blaha turns to Steve and shouts, "Where's your Cav Hat?" Without hesitation, Suiter turns around and dashes back to the remains of his Loach. He reaches inside the wreckage, retrieves his hat, and rushes back to the Huey, all while taking hostile fire from the woods. Once on board, the Huey lifts to a hover, makes a pedal turn to the right, and takes off, flying away from the enemy gunfire as the Huey door gunners fire their M-60 machine guns into the now distant woods.

Sitting in one of the Huey's jump seats, Suiter wears his Cav Hat with a wry smile and a look of stunned elation. The Huey crewmembers glance at Steve, thinking, *That crazy scout pilot just risked his life to rescue his Cav Hat.*

Centaur Scouts (l to r)
1LT Steve Suiter, WO1 Richard Schwab, WO1 Tom Broadbent,
CPT Ron Radcliffe
Photo Courtesy of Steve Suiter

The Smiling Tiger Scouts Hat Band

Warrant Officer John Edmunds arrived in Vietnam in March 1971. He was assigned to C Company, 229th Assault Helicopter Battalion flying Hueys. The 229th was stationed at Bien Hoa Airbase.

John, who had completed the OH-6A transition course before arriving in Vietnam, wanted to fly scout helicopters. He requested a transfer and, in June 1971, joined D Troop, 229th Assault Helicopter Battalion, proudly known as The "Smiling Tigers," flying out of Bearcat Basecamp. There, John served in the scout platoon, flying the Loach with the callsign Tiger 10. It was then that Edmunds placed his order for a Cav Hat.

While eagerly awaiting the delivery of his cavalry hat, John paid close attention to the hats worn by the other Smiling Tiger troopers. When the day finally arrived and his hat was delivered, John carefully removed it from the Stetson box and attached his rank insignia along with shiny brass 229th crossed sabers to the front crown. He then carefully shaped the brim to dip down at both the front and back. At last, John had his cherished cavalry hat.

The Vietnam War Hat Band

In October 1971, the Smiling Tigers relocated from Bearcat to Bien Hoa Airbase. One day, John was browsing the Vietnamese patch store, an on-base concession selling embroidered patches and unit insignia. While there, he discovered a one-inch-wide hat band with red and white stitching that spelled out VIET WAR NAM. As John wrapped the hat band around the crown of his hat, he realized that "WAR" was prominently displayed in the front center, with "Viet" and "Nam" on the sides. *This is perfect*, thought John.

When Edmunds returned to the scout platoon barracks, he was met with a flood of compliments praising his distinctive hat band. Before long, several of the scout pilots were wearing the same hat band, and soon thereafter, the distinctive hat band became the symbol of the scout platoon's identity.

Today, John has his original Cav Hat and hat band on display in his home office. He purchased another Stetson with identical insignia that he wears to reunions as shown in the photo below.

WO1 John Edmunds
Smiling Tiger Scouts
Vietnam – 1971
Photo Courtesy John Edmunds

John Edmunds
2025 VHPA Reunion
St. Louis, MO

Father and Son Cav Hat

Warrant Officer Bob Smith arrived in Vietnam in June 1970 and requested assignment to the 1st Cavalry Division. He was assigned to the 11th Aviation Company, which operated out of Phuoc Vinh, located thirty-two klicks north of Bien Hoa Airbase. The 11th Aviation Company served as the support unit of the 1st Cav, transporting commanders and other officers as needed. Bob flew the OH-6A scout helicopter on single-pilot, no-crew missions.

In October 1970, several troopers from Alpha Troop, 1st of the 9th Cavalry, approached their unit to recruit scout pilots willing to fly the Loach on combat missions. Bob eagerly seized the opportunity and joined Alpha Troop.

From that point on, Smith flew the low bird on pink team missions, covered by a Cobra gunship flying overhead. He typically flew with an observer (oscar) seated in the front and a gunner (torque) in the right side of the rear compartment. Bob remarked, "The Loach was perfect for this mission. It was nimble, had adequate power, and was simple – it had no hydraulics. Plus, it was very crashworthy."

Shortly after joining the 1st of the 9th Cavalry, Bob received his Cav Hat. He proudly wore his distinguished black Stetson whenever he wasn't in the cockpit flying the OH-6A.

After serving six months with Alpha Troop, Bob completed his tour of duty and returned to the United States in early June 1971. Upon arriving in Oakland, California, Smith was given the option to either continue his military career or accept an early conditional release from his military commitment. He opted for early release to complete his college education.

Once Bob settled into civilian life, his cherished Stetson was proudly displayed in a place of honor in his home, where it served as a constant reminder of his military service. When asked about it, Bob would share how incredibly proud he was of serving with the 1st Cavalry. He reflected on this life-changing experience by saying, "I had the privilege of serving alongside some of the most remarkable men I will ever know. I am still in awe of the young, enlisted personnel who crewed those missions, trusting a pilot in his early 20s."

Bob's Son in the Cavalry

Years later, Bob's son enlisted in the Army after graduating from college. Upon completing basic training, Infantry Officer Candidate School (OCS), and jump school, he was assigned to the 2nd Squadron, 7th Cavalry Regiment at Fort Hood, Texas.

In 2008, Bob's son received notice their unit will soon deploy to Iraq. Bob asked his son to wear his Cav Hat, and he eagerly agreed. After a visit to a hat shop in Killeen, Texas, where the hat was cleaned and reshaped, his son wore it during his time in Iraq. A year later, he, along with his Cav Hat and every soldier in his platoon, returned safely.

The Cherished Cav Hat is now displayed in a glass case at his son's home. It features both silver warrant officer and black/gold officer cords. The front crown showcases the crossed sabers of the 1st of the 9th Cavalry, while the rear displays the crossed sabers of the 7th Cavalry along with the Garry Owen insignia.

Bob stated, "I guess my Cav Hat's job wasn't completed with my tour and now has another overseas tour. That hat means the world to me. Every time I see it the memories come flooding back."

Bob Smith's Cav Hat – Front
Note Officer and Warrant Officer Cords
Photo Courtesy of Bob Smith

Bob Smith's Cav Hat – Rear
His Son's 7th Cavalry Brass and
Garry Owen insignia on the Rear Crown
Photo Courtesy of Bob Smith

THE CAV GUY

The Vietnam War Draft Lottery took place on December 1, 1969, for individuals born between 1944 and 1950. At that time, Bill Henry, who was born in 1948, was a student at Central Methodist University (CMU) in Fayette, Missouri. His draft number was eight. Since Bill had secured a student deferment, the draft lottery had no immediate effect.

In May 1970, Bill graduated from CMU, and it wasn't long before he received his draft notice. In compliance with the draft, Henry entered the Army, beginning his training at Fort Leonard Wood, Missouri. He completed Basic Training and subsequently went through Advanced Infantry Training (AIT) at Fort Ord, California, before receiving his orders for Vietnam.

THE "BLUES"

Upon arriving at Bien Hoa Airbase in Vietnam, Specialist Four Bill Henry was assigned to the 1st Cavalry Division and sent to the First Team Academy. He recalls, "Among other things, they taught me to rappel, which was pretty cool."

After completing his training, Bill was assigned to the "Blues" of Alpha Troop, 1st of the 9th Cavalry. The Blues functioned as a small-unit quick reaction force (QRF) that could be deployed by Huey helicopters whenever and wherever needed. Bill explains, "Our typical mission was to support the scouts of the hunter/killer teams when they required ground reconnaissance. We were also called upon to retrieve downed helicopters and to assist the Long-Range Reconnaissance Patrols (LRRPs) when they engaged enemy forces."

During his time with "The Cav," Bill developed a fondness for Cav Hats. While most Apache Troop pilots proudly wore black Stetsons, only a few enlisted troopers could afford them due to their cost. Believe it or not, seventeen dollars was a significant amount of money back then.

One of the enlisted men, Sergeant Craig Little, owned a Cav Hat adorned with a fancy hatband around the crown. Every now and then, Little generously shared his hat with the other enlisted troopers. When it was Bill's turn, he couldn't help but imagine one day owning a Cav Hat.

Returning stateside in January 1972, Bill Henry was released from active duty and readjusted to civilian life. Faced with a pervasive wave of public negativity toward Vietnam veterans, he felt compelled to bury the memories of his military service.

ROLL CALL

For nearly fifty years, Bill carried the heavy burden of suppressed memories and emotions from his time in the Vietnam War. Memories of a once-prideful military service soundly locked away in his subconscious. It was only after settling in Fort Worth, Texas, that he came across a remarkable organization called Roll Call. This inspiring group comprises over 1,000 veterans from all branches and eras of the military, united by a mission to honor and support their fellow servicemen and women.

Roll Call's flagship event is a monthly luncheon held in Fort Worth, which consistently attracts more than five hundred veterans. This gathering serves as a powerful platform for camaraderie, enabling old friends to reconnect while also nurturing new friendships and a renewed sense of belonging. It was there, among newfound brothers-in-arms, that Bill found it was acceptable and personally rewarding to share and be proud of his Vietnam War experiences.

MY STETSON

It was during one of these luncheons, filled with military chatter, laughter, and proud memories of the past, that Bill realized he could finally afford to purchase his revered Cav Hat. He reached out to CavHooah and ordered a Stetson. After attaching his rank, Combat Infantry Badge, and 1st of the 9th crossed sabers, he had the hat steamed and shaped to his liking.

From that moment on, Bill proudly wore his Cav Hat to the Roll Call luncheons. And it wasn't long before Roll Call veterans referred to Bill as "The Cav Guy."

At one of the Roll Call luncheons in 2022, another veteran, Rick Irving, took an inspiring photo of Bill wearing his Cav Hat while saluting the flag during the national anthem. This remarkable photo sealed Bill's identity as The Cav Guy.

Later on, another friend, Collin Kimball, was involved in a historical project for the Frontiers of Flight Museum in Dallas, Texas. To illustrate the evolution of the 9th Cavalry Buffalo Soldiers into the 1st of the 9th Air Cavalry, Collin combined the photo of Bill with an image of a Huey helicopter and a buffalo to create the striking image shown on the follow page.

Bill Henry Saluting the Flag During the National Anthem
Photo Courtesy of Colin Kimball

The Outcasts

CPT Hugh Mills, Author of *Low Level Hell*, (left)
and CPT Rod Willis
Courtesy of Hugh Mills

Captain Hugh Mills hands over command of the Outcasts scout platoon of C Troop, 16th Cavalry, to Captain Rod Willis as Mills prepares to depart Vietnam for the Armor Officer Advanced Course at Fort Knox, Kentucky, in 1972. C Troop was based out of Can Tho Army Airfield in IV Corps.

> **Note:** Captain Willis proudly prepared the Outcasts sign and later realized he misspelled "Aero." To his chagrin, this sign became a running joke within the scout platoon.

Rex Gooch

NOW AND THEN

MAJ (Ret) Ned Ricks – 2023
Vietnam Veterans Memorial Wall

CPT Ned Ricks
Adjutant (S-1), 1st of the 9th Cavalry
F Troop Activation Photo – 1970
Photos Courtesy of Ned B. Ricks

THEN

In response to the success of the air cavalry and the growing demand for cavalry operations, the 1st Squadron (Air), 9th Cavalry, part of the 1st Cavalry Division (Airmobile), expanded in the autumn of 1970 by creating two new troops: Troop E and Troop F. Captain Ned Ricks, the squadron adjutant (S-1), was heavily involved in the personnel aspects of this operation. The photo of Captain Ricks and the F Troop guidon was taken during the troop's inception ceremony.

NOW

At the 2023 Veterans Day event in Naperville, Illinois, the National Veterans Art Museum from Chicago displayed a collection of artwork created by veteran artists, including Major

(Ret.) Ned Ricks. The museum invited Ned to engage with the public, discussing both the artwork and his experiences during the Vietnam War. On this occasion, wearing the Cav Hat was indeed an appropriate choice for headgear.

The highlight of the Veterans Day event was the dedication of a replica of the Vietnam Veterans Memorial Wall, which was funded and created by VFW Chapter 3873. Ned's photo was taken in front of the memorial wall.

"The Cowboys Stole My Cav Hat"

In December 1971, First Lieutenant Russ Van Houten arrived in Vietnam after completing the Cobra gunship transition course at Hunter Army Airfield in Savannah, Georgia. He was assigned to B Troop, 3rd Squadron of the 17th Air Cavalry, affectionately known as "The Stogies," operating out of Phu Loi. Almost immediately, Van Houten began flying combat missions in Cobra gunships.

One of Russ's first and most striking observations was the sight of every B Troop pilot proudly wearing a black cavalry hat. The visual impact was remarkable, and the strong sense of camaraderie among the cavalry troopers was truly inspiring. Motivated by this sense of pride and unity, Russ eagerly ordered his own cavalry hat, wanting to be a part of that proud tradition.

Several weeks later, Russ received his Cav Hat and attached his silver rank insignia and brass crossed sabers to the front crown. It looked impressive, yet it lacked that unique touch that would truly set it apart from other cavalry hats. Russ remarked, "I found a beautifully crafted brass cobra hat pin at a local shop. The pin was circular, about the size of a fifty-cent piece, with the snake coiled inside the circle. The cobra had red ruby eyes that seemed to be looking straight at you. I had never seen another hat pin quite like it. I was proud not only of my cavalry hat but also of the cobra hat pin."

The Trip to Saigon

In February 1972, Russ found himself enjoying a rare day off from flying. It was then that First Lieutenant Dave Simpson, the troop's supply officer and a fellow OCS classmate, approached him with an enticing proposal. Dave invited Russ to join him on a jeep ride to Saigon to pick up much-needed supplies. Without hesitation, Van Houten seized the opportunity, and the two lieutenants set off on their journey toward Saigon, located just twenty klicks to the south.

Along the way, Simpson, who was an enlisted supply sergeant on this first Vietnam tour, suggested they eat lunch in Saigon, as he was familiar with the city and its better restaurants. After enjoying a delightful meal at a Vietnamese restaurant, the two Army officers strolled along the sidewalk on their way back to their jeep.

MY HAT!

Suddenly, Russ felt someone slap him on the back. Instinctively, he turned to see who had hit him, only to have his cavalry hat ripped off his head by two "cowboys" speeding by on motor scooters. There was nothing he could do; the two Vietnamese "cowboys" were already gone.

Russ felt a mix of anger and embarrassment. He regretted not having been more protective of his prized Cav Hat. Nowadays, he jokes that the "cowboys" probably sold the hat to a Viet Cong soldier, who is still wearing it today.

Cobra Hat Pin Similar to Russ's

Charlie Horse Guns

The 3rd Squadron of the 17th Air Cavalry was reactivated at Fort Knox, Kentucky, in November 1966. While stationed there, the squadron concentrated its training on air cavalry tactics centered around observation/gunship teams designed for operations in Southeast Asia.

In November 1967, the 3rd Squadron was deployed to South Vietnam, setting up its headquarters in Di An, which is located approximately nineteen klicks northeast of Saigon. Shortly after their arrival, the squadron was called upon to demonstrate its combat capabilities during the Tet Offensive in January 1968. The 3rd of the 17th Air Cavalry proved to be a formidable opponent in this crucial conflict.

The 3rd Squadron played a crucial role in delivering air cavalry support throughout the western region of the III Corps Tactical Zone. This encompassed a diverse array of operations, including precision attacks, thorough reconnaissance, dynamic air assaults, and vital resupply missions, all essential to maintaining a strategic advantage on the battlefield.

C Troop, also known as Charlie Horse, was commanded by Major Gary Luck. Major Luck was a "soldier's soldier" known for his unwavering dedication to his troops. His commitment to those under his command inspired loyalty and trust, solidifying his reputation as an exemplary cavalry commander.

After the Vietnam War, Luck advanced through the ranks and served in the Gulf War during Operations Desert Shield and Desert Storm, where he commanded the XVIII Airborne Corps. Following a distinguished military career, General Luck retired in 1996 and passed away on August 14, 2024.

This striking photo on the following page captures Major Luck wearing his Cav Hat while he calls Charlie Troop to attention.

Major Gary Luck
Charlie Horse Commanding Officer
Photo Courtesy of Cliff Lawson

In October 1968, a year after the troop's deployment to South Vietnam, the original team of gunship pilots wanted to have their picture taken before several pilots DEROSed and returned to the United States. They asked Captain Cliff Lawson, a gunship pilot and photographer who was then serving as public information officer for 3rd of the 17th Squadron Headquarters, to take their photo. After assembling around one of the troop's Cobra gunships, Cliff took the iconic photo of the Charlie Horse Guns on the following page.

Charlie Horse Guns
C Troop, 3rd of the 17th Air Cavalry
Photo Courtesy of Cliff Lawson

CHAPTER 5
CAV HATS IN IRAQ

In the years following the Vietnam War, the cavalry hat emerged as a symbol of pride and tradition, quickly establishing itself as the esteemed headwear of choice for almost all cavalry units within the United States Army. Its iconic design and Vietnam War battle-tested resilience not only reflect the rich heritage of the cavalry but also serve to unite cavalry troopers under a shared identity and purpose.

The compelling photos and background information in the following chapters vividly depict how the Cav Hat not only bolstered cavalry pride but also paid tribute to the enduring legacy of this esteemed tradition. Moreover, they underscore the profound global presence and influence of the U.S. Cavalry, illustrating its far-reaching impact on the world stage.

> **Note:** Many photos in the following chapters are from the Defense Visual Information Distribution Service and are notated by *DVIDS. "The appearance of U.S. Department of Defense (DoD) visual information does not imply or constitute DoD endorsement."

1st Squadron, 82nd Cavalry Prepares to Deploy
Photo by Specialist Bz Zeller *DVIDS

On May 2, 2009, 1st Squadron, 82nd Cavalry Regiment of the Oregon National Guard was activated for federal service. The 1st Squadron deployed to Iraq from 2009 to 2010, operating as a full reconnaissance unit. It played a crucial role in overseeing security for the Camp Victory Base Complex and Joint Visitors Bureau, as well as safeguarding supply convoys for the forward operating bases in the Baghdad metropolitan area. On June 5, 2010, the squadron was released from active federal service and returned to state control. In recognition of its exemplary service in Iraq, the squadron earned the Meritorious Unit Commendation on July 30, 2010.

In the photo above, 1st Squadron troopers stand in formation during their mobilization ceremony at Mountain View High School in Bend, Oregon. The troops were preparing to depart for Fort Stewart, Georgia, before deployment to Iraq as part of Task Force Stetson, in support of Operation Iraqi Freedom.

COL George Bilafer (left) and CSM Patrick Laidlaw
Stand Next to an AH-64 Apache Attack Helicopter
Photo courtesy of CSM (Ret) Patrick Laidlaw

On August 3, 2003, Colonel George Bilafer assumed leadership of the 11th Attack Helicopter Regiment (AHR) at Balad, Iraq, during Operation Iraqi Freedom. The 11th AHR, proudly bearing the motto "Strike Deep," was comprised of the 2nd of the 6th Cavalry and 6th of the 6th Cavalry Squadrons.

The 11th AHR was responsible for ensuring the security of the main supply route (MSR) from Kuwait to Balad, which served as the Corps Support Activity center for all forces in the theater. Additionally, the regiment provided on-call night security for all forces in the Balad area, to prevent enemy threats to their base of operations.

Command Sergeant Major Patrick Laidlaw, a steadfast senior cavalry NCO, had this to say about Cav Hats: "Cowboys wear hats; as opposed to TRUE CAVALRY TROOPERS that proudly wear STETSONS."

CPT Tiffany Morman, Muleskinner Spur Ride
Photo by Sergeant Ferdinand Thomas *DVIDS

Captain Tiffany Morman, commander of B Company, 115th Brigade Support Battalion – proudly known as the Muleskinners – from Fort Hood, Texas, observes as "Maggots" and spur holders take their places during the Muleskinner's Spur Ride at Camp Taji in Taji, Iraq, on October 18, 2009. Captain Morman designed this year's Spur Ride.

The Spur Ride is an exhaustive rite of passage for aspiring contenders, known as "Maggots," as they strive to earn their coveted silver spurs. This initiation event unfolds over three grueling days, characterized by challenging tasks, intense physical training, and sleep deprivation. It's a transformative experience that tests both physical endurance and mental resilience.

On the climactic final day, Maggots take a celebratory drink from the "Grog" cup, a symbol of camaraderie and resilience. They are then dubbed with silver spurs and presented with a spur holder certificate plaque by one of the Muleskinner spur holders, marking their achievement as a testament to their hard work, dedication, and perseverance.

Cav Hat Unit Crests
Photo by SSG James Selesnick *DVIDS

A cavalry trooper, wearing a cavalry hat adorned with unit crests and insignia, attends a ceremony marking the transition of authority from the 3rd Squadron, 89th Cavalry, 4th Brigade Combat Team, 10th Mountain Division to the 573rd Cavalry, 3rd Brigade Combat Team, 82nd Airborne Division at Forward Operating Base Loyalty in eastern Baghdad, Iraq, on December 30, 2008.

Uncase the Colors
(l to r) LTC Michael McCurry and CSM William McGaha
Photo Courtesy *DVIDS

On March 5, 2011, Lieutenant Colonel Michael McCurry, commander of the 6th Squadron, 17th Cavalry Regiment, and Command Sergeant Major William McGaha from Fort Wainwright, Alaska, uncased the unit's colors during a transfer of authority ceremony held in front of their tactical operations center in northern Iraq.

The 6th Squadron assumed command from the 1st Squadron, 6th Cavalry Regiment. This ceremony marked the conclusion of a month-long relief in place between the two units. The 6-17th Squadron was then responsible for full-spectrum aviation operations in support of stability efforts as part of Operation New Dawn. This unit was expected to be one of the last active-duty U.S. Army units to leave Iraq upon the completion of Operation New Dawn.

Lieutenant Colonel Michael McCurry, 6-17th commander, commented, "Task Force Saber stands ready to carry on with our heritage. Just as F Troop, 17th Cavalry Regiment was the last ground cavalry unit to leave the Republic of Vietnam, so Task Force Saber, with 6th Squadron, 17th Cavalry as its core element, is committed to finishing the mission of Operation New Dawn for the people of Iraq and to honor the efforts that our country has made over the last eight years."[17]

Long Knife Brigade, 1st Cavalry Division
Photo by SPC Creighton Holub *DVIDS

Long Knife Brigade troops wear their Cav Hats during the 1st Cavalry Division's 87th birthday celebration at Contingency Operating Base Adder, near Tallil, Iraq, September 13, 2008.

---

[17] "6-17 Cavalry Begins Iraq Mission." n.d. DVIDS. https://www.dvidshub.net/news/67197/6-17-cavalry-begins-iraq-mission.

At the time of the celebration, the 4th Brigade Combat Team was the only First Team unit deployed overseas. Their mission was to combat smuggling in the southern Iraqi desert border region, reminiscent of the First Team's origins along the U.S.-Mexican border 87 years earlier.

CSM James Pearson (left) and CPT Travis Trammell
Change of Command Ceremony – May 8, 2010
Photo by Specialist David Dyer *DVIDS

Command Sergeant Major James Pearson of the 3rd Heavy Brigade Combat Team received a heartfelt farewell hug from Captain Travis Trammell, the outgoing commander of A Troop, 3rd Squadron, 1st Cavalry Regiment, during a change of command ceremony at Contingency Operating Site Shocker in Iraq on May 8, 2010.

CHAPTER 6
CAV HATS IN AFGHANISTAN

1LT Jeremy A. Woodard, 1-61 Cavalry Regiment
Photo by Sergeant Justin A. Moeller *DVIDS

First Lieutenant Jeremy A. Woodard, a U.S. Army engineer officer with the 1st Squadron, 61st Cavalry Regiment, rides a spirited horse during a dedicated gold spur ceremony at Camp Clark in Afghanistan on October 11, 2013.

A spur ride ceremony is held to induct cavalry troopers into the "Order of the Spur," a time-honored tradition upheld by present-day cavalry units. To earn silver spurs, a cavalry trooper must successfully complete a "spur ride," which tests both their mental and physical fitness. Gold spurs, on the other hand, are awarded for service in combat as a member of a cavalry troop.

On October 11, a special ceremony was held to award gold spurs to troopers who served in combat. Approximately three hundred cavalry troopers from the 1st Squadron, 61st Cavalry Regiment, 4th Brigade Combat Team, 101st Airborne Division (Air Assault) stood in formation at Camp Clark, Afghanistan. They awaited their call for induction into the Order of the Spur, which included donning the gold spurs.

"I earned my first set of gold spurs in Nuristan (Province, Afghanistan), in 2007, but this was my first spur ceremony as the squadron commander," said Lieutenant Colonel Thomas T. Sutton, squadron commander. "We wanted to make this ceremony special, so we brought some horses in to give it a little flavor of the past."

Lieutenant Colonel Sutton shared, "One of the Afghan National Army mechanics who works on the adjoining Afghan National Army (ANA) base, Camp Parsa, was kind enough to lend a few horses for this ceremony, making it even more memorable for the first-time deployers and inductees."[18]

---

[18] "Currahee Cav Receive Gold Spurs." 2013. Www.Army.Mil. October 15, 2013. https://www.army.mil/article/113131/Currahee_Cav_receive_gold_spurs/.

Kellie Pickler
Photo by Corporal Clay Beyersdorfer *DVIDS

Country music singer Kellie Pickler sings while wearing a Stetson cavalry hat given to her by the 2nd Cavalry Regiment during a small concert at Forward Operating Base Walton on December 23, 2013. In this, her seventh USO tour, Kellie visited two countries, performed five shows, and spent time with the troops as part of the "Every Moment Counts" USO campaign.

"The USO tours and programs I've been a part of have definitely been the highlight of my career, so I'm honored to join the USO in helping to raise awareness about the many precious moments that our troops and their families sacrifice due to their commitment and service to our country," Pickler said in a statement. "Every Moment Counts is especially close to my heart because it not only recognizes their personal sacrifices but gives Americans the opportunity to thank our troops with a special gift of a moment."[19]

---

[19] Toomey, Alyssa. 2013. "Kellie Pickler Performs for Troops During 7th USO Tour." E! Online, December 26, 2013. https://www.eonline.com/news/493880/kellie-pickler-performs-for-troops-in-afghanistan-during-7th-uso-tour.

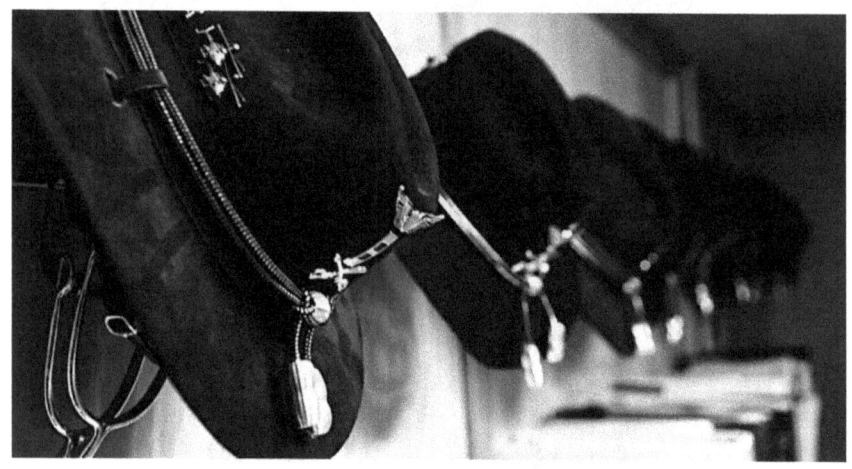

Cav Hats and Spurs
Photo by Staff Sergeant Tracy R. Myers, *DVIDS

Air Cavalry pilots, flying the OH-58D Kiowa Warrior helicopter, from the 101st Combat Aviation Brigade, hang their Stetsons and spurs on the wall during their deployment to Afghanistan. November 6, 2010.

SILVERBELLY CAV HATS RETURN – CRAZYHORSE

In October 2015, Charlie Troop, 3rd of the 17th Cavalry stationed at Fort Hunter-Stewart, Georgia, reflagged from a reconnaissance troop flying OH-58D Kiowa scout helicopters to a heavy attack reconnaissance troop flying the formidable AH-64D Apache gunships. To celebrate their new attack role, Charlie Troop, also known as "Crazyhorse Troop," proudly reintroduced the silverbelly cavalry hats, a tradition first established by their predecessor, Lighthorse Troop, during the Vietnam War.

Note: When Lighthorse Troop stood down in March 1972, it had been reflagged a year earlier from D Troop, 3rd of the 5th Air Cavalry to C Troop, 3rd of the 17th Air Cavalry.

In the lead-up to their deployment to Afghanistan in May 2016, Crazyhorse troopers embraced the silverbelly Cav Hats, wearing them with pride during extensive gunnery and field training operations.

In Afghanistan, Charlie Troop supported Train, Advise, Assist, Command East (TAAC-E) flying attack/reconnaissance missions along the Afghanistan-Pakistan border. They also flew support missions for elite special operations forces. They returned stateside in February 2017.

Charlie Troop returned to Afghanistan in January 2018 for a six-month assignment as part of Taskforce Lighthorse in support of Operations Resolute Support and Freedom's Sentinel. In both Afghanistan deployments, Crazyhorse Troopers proudly wore their silverbelly Cav Hats around the base area and carried their hats with them on combat missions.

For seven years, the Crazyhorse Troopers wore their silverbelly cavalry hats with unwavering pride, symbolizing not just their unique identity but also their deep-rooted heritage.

Sadly, this proud tradition, which defined Crazyhorse as a fierce attack troop, came to a poignant end in 2022. Higher command mandated that Charlie Troop discontinue the esteemed silverbelly Cav Hats and revert to the more traditional black cavalry hats – marking the end of the silverbelly Cav Hat era.

Crazyhorse Apache Gunship Pilots – 2016
Courtesy of CW3 (Ret) Travis Williams

Apache Gunship with Silverbelly Cav Hat in Cockpit
Courtesy of CW3 (Ret) Travis Williams

Crazyhorse Cav Hat in Flight Over Afghanistan – 2016
Photo taken from front seat of Apache Gunship
Courtesy of CW3 (Ret) Travis Williams

Reenlistment Ceremony
(l to r) CSM Maurice Jackson, SGT Jonathan Trivanovich, and
MAJ GEN J. T. Thomson
Photo by SFC Lasonya Morales *DVIDS

The 1st Cavalry Division Sustainment Brigade hosted a mass reenlistment ceremony at Bagram Airfield, Afghanistan, on May 2, 2017. This momentous event celebrated the commitment of seventeen dedicated soldiers, who had the distinct honor of being reenlisted by the commander of the 1st Cavalry Division, Major General J. T. Thomson.

In the picture above, Major General Thomson and Command Sergeant Major Maurice Jackson presented Sergeant Jonathan Trivanovich with a coin and reenlistment certificate.

The 1st Cavalry Division Sustainment Brigade is a divisional logistics and combat support brigade of the United States Army. They deployed to Afghanistan in December 2016.

Case the Colors
COL Cameron Cantlon (left) and CSM Roger Heinze
Photo by Captain Jarrod Morris *DVIDS

Colonel Cameron Cantlon, commander of 3rd Cavalry Regiment, and Command Sergeant Major Roger Heinze carefully fold and case the regimental colors at a ceremony held at Tactical Base Gamberi on February 15, 2015.

The casing of colors marked the end of 3rd Cavalry Regiment "Brave Rifles" mission assigned to Train, Advise, Assist Command – East in eastern Afghanistan. They were replaced by the 3rd Brigade Combat Team "Rakkasans" from the 101st Airborne Division (Air Assault), who assumed the advisory mission and force protection of U.S. coalition troops in eastern Afghanistan.

The 3rd CR deployed to Afghanistan in June 2014, in support of Operation Enduring Freedom. Under OEF the Brave

Rifles performed security force assistance, village support, force protection, and the retrograde and closure of seven forward operating bases.

At the conclusion of the ceremony, the 3rd Brigade Combat Team formally assumed responsibility for training, advising, and assisting corps-level Afghan army and police forces in eastern Afghanistan under NATO's Resolution Support Mission, as well as protecting U.S. coalition forces in the region.[20]

CPT Jamison Pereira, LTC Monte Rone, and CPT Michael Neely
Photo by Specialist Andrew Baker *DVIDS

Captain Jamison Pereira takes over from Captain Michael Neely in a change of command ceremony at Forward Operating

---

[20] "TAAC-E Celebrates 3rd CR Achievements, Rakkasans Begin New Chapter." 2015. Www.Army.Mil. February 16, 2015. https://www.army.mil/article/142926/taac_e celebrates_3rd_cr_achievements_rakkasans_begin_new_chapter.

Base Mehtar Lam, Laghman province, Afghanistan, on March 8, 2013. Captain Pereira assumed command of C Company, 2nd Battalion, 12th Cavalry Regiment, 1st Brigade Combat Team, 1st Cavalry Division.

1st Cavalry Patching Ceremony
BG Viet Luong (left) Patches SGTMatthew Rubin
Photo by Captain Matt McMillan *DVIDS

On February 8, 2015, at Kandahar Airfield in Afghanistan, Brigadier General Viet Luong, commander of the Train, Advise, Assist Command – South, placed a 1st Cavalry Division patch on Sergeant Matthew Rubin's right shoulder. The combat patch ceremony is not just a tradition; it symbolizes a soldier's entitlement to wear their unit patch on the right sleeve, indicating their service with that unit while deployed in a hostile area.

CHAPTER 7
CAV HATS IN EUROPE

Germany Cav Hats

CPT William Rand, K/3-2 Cavalry Regiment
Photo by 1LT Ellen C. Brabo, 2nd Cavalry Regiment *DVIDS

Captain William Rand, the outgoing commander of Kronos Troop, 3rd Squadron, 2nd Cavalry Regiment, salutes the flag during his change of command ceremony at Memorial Field on

Rose Barracks in Germany on April 26, 2019. During the ceremony, Captain Kevin Frey officially assumed command of Kronos Troop.

1st Squadron, 91st Cavalry Trooper – Spur Ride
Photo by Markus Rauchenberger *DVIDS

A cavalry trooper assigned to 1st Squadron, 91st Cavalry Regiment, 173rd Airborne Brigade, proudly wears his Stetson while serving as a lane cadre during a spur ride at the 7th Army Training Command's Grafenwoehr Training Area, Germany, December 11, 2024. The purpose of this spur ride is to integrate new paratroopers into the airborne cavalry and build esprit de corps within the squadron, focused on cavalry heritage.

The 173rd Airborne Brigade was the U.S. Army's Contingency Response Force in Europe, providing rapidly deployable forces to the United States European, African, and Central Command areas of responsibility. Forward deployed across Italy and Germany, the brigade routinely trained alongside NATO allies and partners to build partnerships and strengthen the alliance.

2nd Cavalry Regiment Troopers at War Memorial Rededication Ceremony
Rose Barracks, Vilseck, Germany, July 19, 2018
Photo by Gertrud Zach *DVIDS

Cavalry troopers from the 2nd Cavalry Regiment (2CR) salute during the rededication ceremony of the 2CR War Memorial at Rose Barracks in Vilseck, Germany, on July 19, 2018. This memorial stands as a solemn tribute to the bravery of the

Dragoons, who made the ultimate sacrifice in Iraq and Afghanistan during Operation Iraqi Freedom and Operation Enduring Freedom. Unfortunately, the war memorial was damaged in a storm in June 2017. Thanks to the fundraising efforts of the 2CR Association, the regiment was able to rebuild the memorial.

2nd Cavalry Regiment Troopers
Photo by Sergeant Gianna Elle Sulger *DVIDS

2nd Cavalry Regiment troopers participate in the Change of Command ceremony at Tower Barracks, Grafenwoehr, Germany, May 22, 2024.

This ceremony was held to bid the outgoing regimental commander, Colonel Robert S. McChrystal, farewell and welcome the incoming regimental commander, Colonel Donald R. Neal, Jr.

CSM Dennis Doyle – NCOA's Basic Leader Course
Photo by Sergeant Christian Carrillo *DVIDS

Command Sergeant Major Dennis Doyle of the 2nd Cavalry Regiment delivered remarks to U.S. and multinational soldiers, as well as a U.S. airman, during the graduation ceremony for Class 07-24 of the Noncommissioned Officer Academy (NCOA) Basic Leaders Course.

The ceremony took place in Grafenwoehr, Germany, on June 12, 2024. The NCOA course plays a vital role in shaping future leaders, instilling in them the adaptability and discipline necessary to lead with confidence and effectiveness at the squad and team levels.

Major Cody Cade and Son
U.S. Army National Guard Photo by SSG Lisa Crawford *DVIDS

Major Cody Cade received a heartfelt hug from his five-year-old son, Wyatt, in a touching reunion at Eppley Airfield in Omaha, Nebraska, on January 13, 2024. Family and friends gathered to celebrate the return of ten Nebraska Army National Guard troopers from Headquarters, Headquarters Troop, 1st of the 134th Cavalry Squadron after their ten-month overseas deployment. They served in the U.S. European Command area of responsibility, stationed at Grafenwoehr, Germany, as part of the Joint Multinational Training Group – Ukraine, where they supported training for Ukrainian Armed Forces counterparts.

The Nebraska Soldiers were part of Task Force Bowie – made up of around 160 soldiers in total – which directly trained or supported training for approximately 7,500 Ukrainian troops.

POLAND CAV HATS

CPT Tucker Van-Dyke, Dakota Troop, 4-10 Cavalry Regiment
Photo by 1LT Kimberly Blair *DVIDS

Captain Tucker Van-Dyke, the senior spur holder assigned to Dakota Troop, 4th Squadron, 10th U.S. Cavalry Regiment, part of the 3rd Armored Brigade Combat Team, 4th Infantry Division, observed candidates during a Spur Ride Lane. Dakota Troop executed this rigorous Spur Ride event at the Drawsko Combat Training Center in Poland on July 2, 2024, showcasing their commitment to excellence and combat readiness.

The 3rd Armored Brigade Combat Team, 4th Infantry Division was among other units assigned to 1st Cavalry Division, proudly serving alongside NATO allies and regional security partners to provide combat-credible forces to V Corps, America's forward deployed corps in Europe.

First Sergeant Jefferey Crossman, P Troop, 4-2 Cavalry Regiment
Photo by Captain Spencer Garrison, *DVIDS

A young Polish girl beams with joy as she proudly wears the Stetson of U.S. Army First Sergeant Jefferey Crossman, while sitting beside him at a community outreach event. This memorable gathering took place on August 7, 2015, in Nowa Deba, Poland, bringing together U.S. soldiers from P Troop, 4th Squadron, 2nd Cavalry Regiment to connect and engage with the local community.

This event was an opportunity for the local community to learn more about the visiting American unit. For several weeks, P Troop had been training alongside the Polish army as part of Operation Atlantic Resolve, an ongoing multinational effort to ensure Europe's continued peace and stability through combined training and security cooperation with NATO allies.

2nd Cavalry Regiment Stetson
Photo by Captain John W. Strickland *DVIDS

A cavalry Stetson belonging to a Mustang Trooper of the 2nd Cavalry Regiment sits on top of their equipment after arriving in Suwalki, Poland, during Saber Strike 17 on June 17, 2017. This operation was a U.S. Army Europe-led multinational combined forces exercise conducted annually to enhance the NATO Alliance throughout the Baltic region and Poland.

Saber Strike 17 featured rigorous integrated and synchronized training focused on deterrence, significantly enhancing the interoperability and readiness of the military forces from all twenty participating nations.

The Poland-based Forward Presence Battle Group conducted the convoy portion of the Field Training Exercise to demonstrate their ability to execute a forward passage of lines across the only land connection between the Baltic States of Estonia, Latvia, and Lithuania, which is known as the Suwalki Gap.

Sergeant Zachary McDavis, Cavalry Scout
1st Squadron, 1st Cavalry Regiment
Photo by Specialist Trevares Johnson *DVIDS

In a lively atmosphere filled with cheers and camaraderie, cavalry scouts from the 1st Squadron, 1st Cavalry Regiment, 2nd Armored Brigade Combat Team, 1st Armored Division gathered to honor and celebrate the 191-year legacy of their squadron on March 2, 2024.

The 1st Squadron, 1st Cavalry Regiment, proudly known as the "Blackhawks," commemorated nearly two centuries of exemplary service to our nation upon successfully concluding its mission in Jaworze, Poland. With an unwavering commitment to excellence, the squadron navigates the dynamic challenges of modern global warfare and stands prepared to confront any threat at a moment's notice.

CSM Sheldon Watson, 1-9 Cavalry Regiment
Photo by SGT Cesar Salazar Jr. *DVIDS

On September 4, 2023, U.S. Army Command Sergeant Major Sheldon Watson, the senior enlisted advisor for the 1st Battalion, 9th Cavalry Regiment of the 1st Cavalry Division, which was supporting the 4th Infantry Division, met the horse he would ride during an esprit de corps event in Kierzbuń, Poland. This event, attended by the leadership of the unit, served to honor the longstanding traditions of the cavalry while also facilitating meaningful farewell celebrations, reinforcing the commitment and unity among the members of the regiment.

The mission of the 4th Infantry Division in Europe was to engage in multinational training and exercises across the continent, collaborating with NATO allies and regional security partners to provide combat-ready forces to V Corps, America's forward deployed corps in Europe.

SLOVAKIA CAV HATS

Cavalry Stetson in Slovakia
U.S. Air National Guard photo by SrA Jonathan W. Padish *DVIDS

A cavalry Stetson hat rests on the lap of U.S. Army Specialist Claudio Rentas, a cavalry scout with the 1st Squadron, 152nd Cavalry Regiment, 76th Infantry Brigade Combat Team, 38th Infantry Division, Indiana Army National Guard. Rentas was in transit to Slovakia as part of Slovak Shield 2019 on October 27, 2019.

Slovak Shield 2019 was a military field training exercise involving five NATO countries designed to promote joint interoperability and foster cross-national collaboration. The training focused on urban warfare – an area of operations in which the 1-152nd Cavalry typically does not engage. During this exercise, troopers seized the opportunity to acquire new skills and knowledge while working alongside their Slovak counterparts.

CROATIA CAV HATS

MAJ Nenad Vecenaj and CSM Sean Allison
U.S. Army National Guard photo by SGT John Schoebel *DVIDS

Major Nenad Vecenaj, the outgoing commander of the 10th Croatian Contingent, Thunder, presents a challenge coin to U.S. Army Command Sergeant Major Sean Allison. Command Sergeant Major Allison serves as the command sergeant major of Battle Group Poland and the 3rd Battalion, 8th Cavalry Regiment, part of the 3rd Armored Brigade Combat Team in the 1st Cavalry Division. This exchange took place during the Hand Over/Take Over ceremony held in Bemowo Piskie, Poland, on January 24, 2023.

The Croatian army was proudly working alongside the 1st Infantry Division, NATO allies, and regional security partners to provide combat-credible forces to V Corps, under America's forward deployed corps in Europe.

HUNGARY CAV HATS

Apache Troop Cav Hat
Photo by CPT John Strickland, *DVIDS

Apache Troop of the 4th Squadron, 10th Cavalry Regiment, executed a spur ride from May 30 to June 1, 2017, in Tata, Hungary. This event reinforced the collaboration with their Hungarian allies and provided a thorough evaluation of the troopers' cavalry skills. Beyond skill assessment, the ride fostered strong camaraderie among the troops and their partners, reinforcing bonds that transcend borders. It also offered an exceptional opportunity for troopers to earn the prestigious silver spurs, a symbol of pride in cavalry service.

Apache troop was deployed to Hungary in support of Operation Atlantic Resolve, a U.S.-led effort to strengthen the alliance and demonstrate its commitment to NATO.

Finland Cav Hats

CPT Jose Mäntäylä and LTC Levi Thompson
Photo by Specialist Charles Leitner *DVIDS

On November 5, 2022, U.S. Army Lieutenant Colonel Levi Thompson proudly presented Finnish Captain Jose Mäntäylä with the cavalry unit's iconic Stetson during a distinguished ceremony. This event was a highlight of Hammer 22, an annual combined forces exercise that brings together Finland's Army Headquarters, the Armored Brigade, the Pori Brigade, the Karelia Brigade, the Utti Jaeger Regiment, and the Logistics Department of the Defense Forces. This impressive exercise takes place in Niinisalo, Finland.

Lieutenant Colonel Thompson was the commander of the 6th Squadron, 9th Cavalry Regiment, 3rd Armored Brigade Combat Team, 1st Cavalry Division, which was operationally assigned to the 1st Infantry Division. The 1st Infantry Division proudly worked alongside allies and regional security partners to provide combat-credible forces to V Corps in Europe.

CHAPTER 8
SQUADRON & REGIMENT CAV HATS

Note: In accordance with the Secretary of Defense Directive issued on April 30, 2025, the Army Transformation Initiative (ATI) was introduced to prioritize fighting formations that directly contribute to lethality. "To achieve this, ATI comprises three lines of effort: deliver critical warfighting capabilities, optimize our force structure, and eliminate waste and obsolete programs."

To optimize force structure within Army Aviation, the ATI announced, "We will also restructure Army Aviation by reducing one Aerial Cavalry Squadron per Combat Aviation Brigade (CAB) in the Active Component, and we will consolidate aviation sustainment requirements and increase operational readiness."[21] Several of the Air Cavalry Squadrons featured in this chapter have received notification of deactivation and/or transformation into a Combat Aviation Brigade.

---

[21] "Letter to the Force: Army Transformation Initiative." 2025. Www.Army.Mil. May 2, 2025. https://www.army.mil/article/285100/letter_to_the_force_army_transformation_initiative.

3ʀᴅ Cavalry Regiment – Brave Rifles

The Regiment of Mounted Riflemen was authorized by an act of Congress in 1846, bringing into existence a new organization in the American Army: a regiment of riflemen, mounted for greater mobility than the infantry. Equipped with percussion rifles, the Mounted Riflemen could fire at greater distances and with more accuracy than the muskets of the infantry or the dragoon's smooth-bore carbines.

> **Note:** In homage to the cavalry of yesteryear, the 3ʳᵈ Cavalry Regiment adopts a classic writing style from the 1800s by omitting the "r" in 3ʳᵈ. So, in honor of this proud tradition, this narrative will also refer to the 3d Cavalry Regiment.

Mexican War, "Brave Rifles"

It was in the Mexican War in 1847 that the regiment earned its moniker of "Brave Rifles" and adopted its motto of "Blood and Steel." According to legend, the men of the regiment were bloodied and exhausted after fierce fighting at Chapultepec. When General Winfield Scott approached and saw each soldier rise to attention, he was so moved by their display of valor that he removed his hat, bowed, and proclaimed, "Brave Rifles!

Veterans! You have been baptized in fire and blood and have come out steel!"

Major General Winfield Scott
Engraved by T. B. Welch, 1846
Courtesy of Library of Congress

CIVIL WAR

When the Civil War broke out, the regiment of Mounted Riflemen was assigned to the New Mexico Territory, where it fought against both Apache Indians and Confederate Texans. In August 1861, an act of Congress officially transitioned the regiment from mounted riflemen to the 3d United States Cavalry.

In 1862, the regiment participated in the Battles of Valverde and Glorietta Pass in New Mexico. Moving eastward in 1863, the regiment fought in Tennessee, Mississippi, Alabama, and North Carolina as part of the advance guard for Sherman's Army. After the war, the regiment returned to New Mexico and later moved to Arizona, where it continued to engage with the Apaches.

SPANISH-AMERICAN WAR

When war broke out with Spain near the close of the nineteenth century, the regiment was dispatched to Tampa, Florida, for training before the invasion of Cuba. It was during this time in Florida that a remarkable event unfolded, which would shape the identity and legacy of the cavalry for generations to come.

OLD BILL

In 1898, American artist Frederic Remington was visiting the camp of the 3d U.S. Cavalry in Tampa, Florida, where the regiment was preparing for the invasion of Cuba. While there, Remington's attention was drawn to one of the troop's noncommissioned officers, Sergeant John Lannen. A superb rider and an imposing figure, Lannen impressed Remington as the epitome of the cavalryman. With the troop commander's approval, the artist made several rough sketches of the white-haired, white-mustached sergeant.

From the initial sketches, Remington later created the well-known drawing of a trooper mounted on his horse, wearing a model 1883 campaign hat, and cradling a carbine in his arms. At some point, this drawing became known as "Old Bill." It represents a trooper, a military unit, and a branch of service, ultimately symbolizing mobile operations in the U.S. Army.

Who was the man who served as the model for the Remington sketch? At the time he posed, Sergeant John Lannen was nearing thirty years of service and looking forward to retirement. This blue-eyed, ruddy-complexioned soldier was highly respected by his officers, known as an outstanding sergeant who was loyal to his superiors. He was a stern disciplinarian but maintained unfailing good humor even under challenging conditions. Lannen was a gallant man and a noncommissioned officer of the old-fashioned kind, whose orders were always obeyed.

Tragically, Sergeant Lannen contracted yellow fever, as did so many other Americans in the war. He died in Santiago soon after the campaign ended, mere days before he was set to retire.

Old Bill by Frederic Remington

During the Santiago Campaign, three troops of the 3d Cavalry Regiment participated in the famous assault on San Juan Heights.

PHILIPPINES

After the war, the regiment was ordered to the Philippines to assist in quelling the insurrection there. It fought sixty-two engagements from October 1899 to 1902.[22]

PRESENT DAY – NATIONAL TRAINING CENTER

Based at Fort Hood, Texas, the regiment deployed to the National Training Center (NTC) in August 2023 for another historic clash, this time between the 3d Cavalry Regiment and the 11th Armored Cavalry Regiment (11th ACR), fighting as the "North Torbian" enemy. In a first for the 3d Cavalry Regiment, the Republic of Korea Army Forces were integrated to form a Combined Joint Regimental Task Force.

During the battle, the 3d Cavalry Regiment was baptized in blood, fire, and a hurricane! After completing a forty-kilometer road march to the western Tactical Assembly Areas, the regiment seized the passes in a bloody battle, liberated Osu-Dong and Jin-Dong, and executed a regimental live fire, all while enduring the remnants of Hurricane Hilary, the largest storm to hit California in eighty-four years. The rotation concluded with an epic Lucky 16 where 11th ACR and 3d Cavalry troopers gathered under seventy red, white, and gold guidons and standards to celebrate their cavalry heritage until the next ride!

KOREA DEPLOYMENT

In the winter of 2024, the 3d Cavalry Regiment deployed to South Korea to serve as the Korea Rotational Force (KRF14). Twelve hours after uncasing their colors on February 29, 2024,

---

[22] "3d Cavalry Regiment History: U.S. Army Fort Hood." n.d. https://home.army.mil/hood/units-tenants/3cr/3d-cavalry-regiment-history.

the regiment conducted its first alert and fired the first rounds twenty-four hours later at the Rodriquez Live Fire Complex.

Then, the first theater-level exercise commenced forty-eight hours later. During the exercise, the 3d Cavalry Regiment demonstrated lethality and readiness while participating in multiple exercises and live fires, including the first air assault deployment of an expeditionary Regimental Tactical Operations Center (RTOC) to the Demilitarized Zone, and the largest international multi-echelon joint, Combined Arms Live Fire Exercise (CALFEX) in KRF history. During this extensive exercise, 183 3d Cavalry troopers and sixty-two Republic of Korea (ROK) Allies earned E3B badges (Expert Soldier Badge (ESB), Expert Infantry Badge (EIB), and Expert Field Medical Badge (EFMB). On October 25, 2024, the 3d Cavalry Regiment cased the standards and redeployed to Fort Cavazos (Now Fort Hood), Texas.

RECENT TIMES

In 2025, the regiment deployed the lead elements of Task Force Sabre to support Cadet Command's Cadet Summer Training in April. In May, the regiment held its annual Brave Rifles week, also celebrating the 80th anniversary of victory in World War II and the regiment's 179th birthday. At this time, Pioneer Squadron was inactivated, ending its 10-year service in the 3d Cavalry Regiment.

At the time of this publication, a significant Army transformation is underway, which will lead to future changes in the regiment as an armored formation. As always, troopers of this regiment lean on the history of this proud regiment and stand Brave Rifles Tough, ready to write the next chapter.

Colonel Jeffrey Barta, 3d Cavalry Regiment Commander
Assumes Command of the 14th Korean Rotational Force
Camp Casey, South Korea, Feb. 29, 2024
Photo by Chin-U Pak *DVIDS

3d Cavalry Brave Rifles Week – 2025
M777 Towed Howitzer demonstation
Photo by Scott Darling *DVIDS

3d Cavalry Regiment CSM Mikeal McInroy
Awards Ceremony – September 15, 2023
Photo by Sergeant Alex Romey *DVIDS

CHARGE!
3d Cavalry Regimental Run – July 11, 2023
Photo by Sergeant Alex Romey *DVIDS

11ᵗʰ Armored Cavalry Regiment – Blackhorse

After achieving victory in the Spanish-American War of 1898, the United States faced the new challenge of Territorial Administration. The responsibility fell primarily to the regular Army, which was found to be undermanned for this mission. In response, Congress decided to increase the standing Army by adding five infantry regiments and five cavalry regiments. Consequently, on February 2, 1901, the 11th Cavalry Regiment became the first of the five newly established cavalry regiments. This was followed by the formation of the 12th, 13th, 14th, and 15th Cavalry Regiments.

The 11th Cavalry Regiment's first military engagement occurred when the regiment deployed to the Philippines in early 1902 as part of the Philippine-American War. In photographs from that time, the 11th Cavalry troopers wore the Model 1883 Campaign Hat in what appears to be a mid-shade of brown. The hat complemented the uniform, which consisted of a dark blue chambray shirt paired with buff-colored khaki trousers. Canvas leggings were worn over low-cut boots. For field use, a khaki jacket was issued, while a dark blue coat was reserved for formal occasions.[23]

---

[23] The Blackhorse Association. 2018. "11th Armored Cavalry Regiment History - the Blackhorse Association." September 27, 2018. https://blackhorse.org/11th-armored-cavalry-regiment-history/.

Trooper Adolphus McGill
1st Squadron, 11th Cavalry, 1906
Courtesy Blackhorse Association

11th Cavalry Trooper in Cuba, 1907
Courtesy Blackhorse Association

THE LAST CHARGE – 11TH CAVALRY REGIMENT

On May 5, 1916, after a grueling thirty-six-mile, all-night march – much of which at the trot – the Provisional Squadron, under the determined leadership of Major Robert Howze, surprised a band of approximately two hundred Villistas at the Ojos Azules ranch. The lead Apache scouts sighted the bandits, dismounted, and took them under fire. In a bold and decisive maneuver, A Troop swiftly transformed from their march column into a column of fours and charged. The follow-on troops mirrored this action, skillfully alternating to the right and left as they broke free from the march column. Meanwhile, G Troop assumed the critical role of squadron reserve, ready to support and reinforce the advance.

By the end of the Cinco de Mayo battle, only one trooper from the 11th Cavalry was injured, while the Mexican forces suffered over fifty fatalities and the capture of several key leaders.

The action at Ojos Azules marked the last mounted charge in the history of the United States Cavalry and was also the first combat use of the Colt .45 automatic pistol. General John J. Pershing later called this action a "brilliant piece of work."[24]

"Last Charge"
Painting by Don Stivers
Courtesy of donstivers.com

The "Last Charge" painting by Don Stivers superbly depicts the cavalry charge with the 11th Cavalry troopers wearing Model 1883 campaign hats and firing the Colt .45 automatic pistol.

---

[24] Snedeker, Don, historian, 11th Armored Cavalry Veterans of Vietnam and Cambodia, 2025.

THE 11ᵀᴴ ARMORED CAVALRY REGIMENT TODAY

On October 15, 1993, the 11th Armored Cavalry Regiment was deactivated as part of a reduction of forces in Europe. Then, on October 16, 1994, the regiment was reactivated in Fort Irwin, California, as the opposing force for the National Training Center. Upon reactivation, the regimental commander, Colonel Terry Tucker, resurrected the brown campaign hats of yesteryear as they assumed this critical mission as the "World Class OPFOR" (opposing force). The hats worn today are patterned after the 1883 campaign hat and manufactured by Greeley Hat Works. The brown campaign hats are further discussed in Chapter 10 – Cav Hat Creases and Brims.

11th ACR Brown Campaign Hat

11th Armored Cavalry Regiment and Brown Campaign Hats
- The 11th ACR is currently the only U.S. Army unit that wears the brown campaign hat.
- All grades are authorized to wear the brown hat; however, it is most commonly bought and worn by senior NCOs and officers.
- The brown campaign hat is worn at all official functions and on the last workday of each week. It is also worn by the troopers in the ceremonial Horse Detachment.

- The Blackhorse Association has partnered with Greeley Hat Works to sell the brown campaign hats on the association's website.
- Well respected and recognized as a highly effective combat force, Blackhorse routinely defeats Armored Brigade Combat Teams twice their size during rotations at NTC, despite the 11th ACR using older equipment.
- The 11th Armored Cavalry Regiment is genuinely in a league of their own when it comes to cavalry, and the distinctive brown campaign hat is one of many things that set them apart from the rest of the Army.

Photos are courtesy of the 11th Armored Cavalry Regiment Public Affairs Office, Fort Irwin, California.

11th ACR Change of Command
CSM David L. Shipman (left) Receiving Guidon From
COL Kevin T. Black

Charge!
11th Armored Cavalry Regiment Horse Detachment

Horse Detachment Color Guard
Change of Command Ceremony – June 28, 2018

1ST SQUADRON, 17TH CAVALRY REGIMENT

Based at Fort Bragg, North Carolina, 1st Squadron, 17th Cavalry Regiment traces its origins to Troop A of the 17th Cavalry Regiment, which was activated on July 1, 1916. The regiment was established with a cadre of experienced soldiers from the 1st, 3rd, 6th, 8th, and 14th Cavalry Regiments at Fort Bliss, Texas. For the next three years, Troop A and the 17th Cavalry patrolled the United States-Mexico border in Texas and Arizona. In 1919, the entire regiment was reorganized and deployed to Hawaii to serve as a mobile force, ensuring the protection of the islands' coastline.

In the aftermath of World War I, the 17th Cavalry Regiment was called back to the mainland and officially inactivated at the historic Presidio of Monterey in California on September 26, 1921.

In 1942, during World War II, a squadron was formed and assigned to the 82nd Airborne Division. In April of that year, it was redesignated as the 82nd Cavalry Reconnaissance Troop. The troop was credited with missions in northern France, the Rhineland, Ardennes-Alsace, and Central Europe. In December 1947, the troop was reorganized, redesignated, and relieved of its assignment to the 82nd Airborne Division.

FROM HORSES TO HELICOPTERS

On September 1, 1957, the squadron reestablished its affiliation with the 82nd Airborne Division when Troop A, 17th Cavalry, was reactivated, at Fort Bragg, North Carolina. It became one of the first divisional cavalry and reconnaissance troops equipped with helicopters.

RECENT TIMES

In 1993, the 1st Squadron, 17th Cavalry upgraded its aircraft fleet to include OH-58D(I) helicopters and retired the last Cobra AH-1F gunship on June 21, 1993. The Aviation Resource Initiative (ARI) mandated that the squadron maintain a pure aircraft fleet, resulting in the deactivation of E Troop (UH-60 Blackhawk), which was subsequently reflagged as the squadron's Maintenance Troop. The events of September 11, 2001, marked a significant turning point for the squadron, as it began preparing for its role in the War on Terror.

From 2002 to 2024, the 1-17 Cavalry Regiment consistently deployed in support of both Operation Enduring Freedom and Operation Iraqi Freedom, demonstrating a remarkable commitment to global contingency operations. The squadron undertook a wide range of missions, including air assaults, reconnaissance, security operations, and critical resupply. Throughout multiple deployments to both Afghanistan and Iraq – often operating under the designations Task Force SABER or PALEHORSE – the unit built a reputation for professionalism and exceptional performance.

The regiment underwent a substantial transformation during this period, evolving from a Kiowa Warrior Squadron into a formidable Heavy Attack Reconnaissance Squadron. This evolution was marked by the integration of AH-64D and subsequently AH-64E Apache helicopters, along with the RQ-7B Shadow unmanned aircraft system (UAS), significantly enhancing its operational capabilities and readiness.

On September 27, 2023, Task Force Nighthawk, headquartered by Task Force Saber, was activated to deploy to the Central Command Area of Responsibility (CENTCOM AOR) in support of Combined Joint Task Force – Operation Inherent Resolve, to assist partner forces and deter and defeat the Da'esh in Iraq.

With an eye toward its lineage and traditions of the past, the squadron epitomizes its motto: **FORWARD!**

1-17 Cavalry Pass in Review with Apache Gunships Overhead
Change of Command Ceremony, July 10, 2025
Photo Courtesy of 2LT Jeyra Resto Calero

LTC Christopher Wardlaw, Saber 6
Addresses the Formation, Erbil, Iraq, 2024
Photo by SGT Vincent Levelev *DVIDS

1-17 Cavalry Stetson Inside OH-58 Windscreen in Rain
Aerial Gunnery Training at Camp Lejeune, NC, March 2015
Photo by Captain Adan Cazarez *DVIDS

2ND SQUADRON, 17TH CAVALRY REGIMENT

Based out of Fort Campbell, Kentucky, the 2nd Squadron, 17th Cavalry Regiment, now known as the 2-17 Air Cavalry Squadron, originated in 1916 during World War I. Throughout its long history of excellence, the squadron has evolved from riding horseback to flying helicopters. However, their mission remains unchanged: to advance ahead of the main forces, observe the battlefield, report findings, and take action when necessary.

The 2nd Squadron, 17th Cavalry, was first deployed to Vietnam in December 1967, serving as the ground cavalry squadron of the 101st Airborne Division. As the division transitioned to airmobile operations, the squadron converted to an air cavalry squadron between December 1968 and June 1969. Chapter 4 features several compelling stories that highlight the 2-17 Air Cavalry troopers and their Cav Hats.

During the initial Vietnam ground deployment, the squadron was commanded by Lieutenant Colonel Julius W. Becton, who later rose to the rank of lieutenant general. The soldiers participated in operations around Bien Hoa and then Song Be during Tet of 1968. Then, in February, they deployed north to Thuy Thien Provence in support of Operation Pegasus to relieve Marines under siege at Khe Sanh. It was there that the squadron conducted a successful blocking operation along the infamous "Street Without Joy," a vast expanse of terrain east of Highway 1, stretching from Quang Tri to Hue.

The troops achieved remarkable success, defeating scores of enemy combatants while exhibiting numerous acts of exceptional bravery. Three of the twenty Medal of Honor recipients from the 101st Airborne Division were troopers in the 2nd Squadron, 17th Cavalry Regiment. They are Sergeant Robert M. Patterson, Specialist 4 Joseph G. LaPointe Jr., and Specialist 4 Michael J. Fitzmaurice.

Recent Operations

After the Vietnam War, the squadron transitioned from the OH-6A Cayuse to the OH-58D Kiowa Warrior helicopter. This small, agile aircraft enabled pilots to fly close to the terrain, maintain communication with ground forces, and provide immediate support when it mattered most.

In 2015, the Army retired the Kiowa fleet, and the 2nd Squadron, 17th Cavalry Regiment, transitioned to the AH-64 Apache. This new aircraft offered increased firepower, greater survivability, and advanced sensors. Despite the significant changes in the platform, the mission remained consistent.

In January 2025, the 2nd of the 17th Air Cavalry deployed to Iraq and were based out of Erbil Airbase, as part of Operation Inherent Resolve. The squadron collaborated with joint and partner units throughout the operational area to conduct reconnaissance flights aimed at identifying potential threats. These missions offered direct support during ground movements and ensured that commanders maintained constant visibility of the operational environment. The squadron played a vital role in the operation by helping to maintain stability, restricting the enemy's freedom of movement, and protecting personnel on the ground.

While stationed at Erbil Airbase, the squadron hosted a rigorous two-day Spur Ride on April 28, 2025. Of the sixty-six determined "Shavetails" who embarked on this mentally demanding and physically challenging journey, fifty-six emerged triumphant, earning their coveted silver spurs. The photos below are of spur holders supervising and organizing the event.

The troopers of the 2nd Squadron, 17th Cavalry Regiment strive to uphold their motto: Always **"Out Front."**

1SG Julio Macias   CPT Hunter Purvis

2-17 Cav Hat at Spur Ride
Photo Courtesy of MSG Ray Boyington

CW4 Glenn Stewart's Stetson Over Iraq – May 2025
Proudly Displaying Dirt from Iraq, Afghanistan, Kuwait,
South Korea, and Germany
Photo Courtesy of CW4 Glenn Stewart

Promotion Ceremony, Currahee Mountain, GA, Oct. 7, 2025
Saber 6, LTC Mark Conklin (left) Promoted:
(l to r) CPT Abigail Metje, CW3 Kevin Hopson, CW2 Sean Kelly
Photo Courtesy of LTC Mark Conklin

3ʳᴅ Sǫᴜᴀᴅʀᴏɴ, 17ᵀᴴ Cᴀᴠᴀʟʀʏ Rᴇɢɪᴍᴇɴᴛ

Since the Vietnam War Era, the 3ʳᵈ of the 17ᵗʰ Air Cavalry Squadron has seen significant combat action in the following operations:

- Somalia, 1992 – Operation Restore Hope
- Iraq, 2003 – Operation Iraqi Freedom, where the squadron earned the Meritorious Unit Commendation for operations in Samarra, Mosul, and Tal Afar. It was during this operation that the squadron assumed the name "Lighthorse."
- Iraq, 2007 – "The Surge" where the squadron served to secure the "Southern Belts" of Baghdad.
- Afghanistan, 2011 – Lighthorse was again awarded the Meritorious Unit Commendation for duties performed while operating out of Jalalabad.
- 2016 – The squadron transitioned from OH-58 scout helicopters to AH-64D gunships and assumed an attack gunship role. Several months later, Charlie Troop deployed to Bagram Airfield, Afghanistan, in support of Operation Freedom's Sentinel.

Tʜᴇ Sǫᴜᴀᴅʀᴏɴ Tᴏᴅᴀʏ

Based at Hunter Army Airfield in Savannah, Georgia, the 3ʳᵈ Squadron, 17ᵗʰ Cavalry Regiment, nicknamed Lighthorse, has undergone significant transformation throughout the years. What has remained constant, however, is Lighthorse's readiness to adapt to the changes in warfare the Army sees necessary to fight and win future conflicts.

Currently, the squadron consists of:
- Headquarters and Headquarters Troop (Red Horse)
- Alpha Troop (Silver Spurs)
- Bravo Troop (Blackjack)
- Charlie Troop (Crazyhorse)
- Delta Troop (Blue Tigers)
- Echo Troop (Enforcers)
- Fox Troop (Centaurs)
- Echo Company, 3rd Aviation Regiment (Cerberus)

Lighthorse Troopers currently sport the AH-64E Apache Guardian and the MQ-1 Gray Eagle, fulfilling a wide variety of roles in direct support of the Ground Force commander. In years past, the squadron fielded the AH-64D Apache Longbow, the OH-58 A/C Kiowa Warrior, and the legacy AH-1 Cobra, UH-1 Huey, and OH-6 Cayuse (Loach).

Recent Operations

As combat operations within the Army – and more broadly, the entire Department of Defense – have begun to draw down, the 3rd of the 17th Air Cavalry Squadron has remained versatile. In a departure from its rich history in combat operations, the squadron's expeditionary activities in the current decade have focused on training alongside NATO allies in deterring the growing threat of Russian aggression. Most recently, Lighthorse deployed to Europe in 2023 in support of Operation Atlantic

Resolve, and Echo Company, 3rd Aviation Regiment, deployed as part of Joint Task Force – Southern Border from February to March 2025.

Gunnery Training

While stateside, Lighthorse remains operationally ready and continues to train for the demands of Large-Scale Combat Operations (LSCO). A bulk of this is accomplished through conducting aerial gunnery exercises, field deployments, and deployments to Combat Training Centers such as the National Training Center in Fort Irwin, California. During these exercises, pilots are evaluated on the employment of the various weapons systems of the AH-64E and their techniques.

Additionally, tactical scenarios are developed to evaluate the planning abilities of aircrews and leadership in an imagined LSCO environment.

Another layer of realism and complexity is added as gunnery exercises are often conducted under austere conditions while deployed in a field environment, simulating the harsh environment of combat deployments. This places great emphasis on planning factors such as maintenance supplies and logistics movement, which often increases stress and fatigue due to environmental factors.

Future Readiness

As the 3rd of the 17th Air Cavalry Squadron continues to adapt to the constant changes in the Army, the Department of Defense, and the world, Lighthorse has also remained true to its time-honored traditions and heritage. Just as with the cavalry troopers of old, the Stetson or Cav Hat is a mark of unit identity and spurs the mark of individual professionalism and pride. The

Lighthorse Troopers regularly conduct ceremonies where a Stetson must be "broken in" before it is worn – the only requirement being that a trooper has supplied their own Stetson. Meanwhile, the squadron conducts annual Spur Rides where troopers are afforded the opportunity to demonstrate their prowess to earn their spurs in a way that instills pride in the cavalry heritage and builds camaraderie with fellow soldiers.

It is an often-repeated irony that the only thing constant in the Army is change. While Lighthorse has played a significant role in spearheading change in recent years, they have solidified a new constant in their proud tradition.

Lighthorse Squadron has been notified they will deactivate on October 15, 2025, and transform into 1st of the 3rd Attack Battalion. Lighthorse will host a final Spur Ride in the spring of 2026.

CW2 Aaron Sargent (left) and CPT Lauren Smart
walk to their AH-64 Apache for aerial gunnery training.
3-17 Cavalry, Hunter Army Airfield, GA, Nov. 2, 2021
Photo by SGT Andrew McNeil *DVIDS

CPT Lauren Smart, an Apache pilot, prepares for flight.
3-17 Cavalry, Hunter Army Airfield, Georgia, Nov. 2, 2021
Photo by SGT Andrew McNeil *DVIDS

5ᵀᴴ Squadron, 17ᵀᴴ Cavalry Regiment

Based out of Camp Humphreys in the Republic of Korea, the 5ᵗʰ of the 17ᵗʰ Air Cavalry Squadron (5-17 ACS) traces its lineage to Troop E, 17ᵗʰ Cavalry Regiment, formed at Fort Bliss, Texas, in 1916. Throughout its long history of excellence, the squadron has evolved from riding horseback to flying Apache helicopters and drones. Despite this evolution, their mission has remained consistent: to advance ahead of the main force, observe the battlefield, report on enemy movements, and engage the enemy when necessary.

Recent Operations

In July 2024, 5-17 ACS, also known as Saber Squadron, executed a Combined Arms Live Fire Exercise (CALFEX) at Rodriguez Live Fire Complex in support of the 3ʳᵈ Cavalry Regiment. During this exercise, Saber Squadron executed nearly eighty iterations on the range alongside 3ʳᵈ Cavalry Strykers, M777 artillery, 120mm mortars, Korean Army tanks, and USAF A-10 Warthogs. Saber aircrews logged more than 150 flight hours supporting the "Brave Rifles" of the 3ʳᵈ Cavalry.

In September, 5-17 ACS conducted Operation Saber Storm, which simulated an emergency deployment. This operation included Apache simulator missions, convoy rehearsals, and a final event where the squadron deployed to a field site near Rodriguez Range. Aircrews carried out reconnaissance missions near the Korean DMZ, and the squadron executed its first-ever flight with a small unmanned aircraft system (UAS), commonly known as a drone. Throughout the operation, the entire squadron gained valuable insights into command and control in a challenging environment, emphasizing the importance of communication and refining mobile command post concepts.

In October, 5-17 ACS executed aerial gunnery training at Rodriguez Range as Task Force Saber. The task force completed Gunnery Table VI (crew qualification), Gunnery Table IX (platoon qualification), and combined tables with the Republic of Korea (ROK) 901st Apache Battalion.

In January and February 2025, 5-17 ACS returned to Rodriguez Range to support a Stryker Brigade Combat Team for company live fire and a CALFEX. The squadron focused on long-range lethality by launching aircraft from Camp Humphreys and traveling hundreds of miles each day to engage targets for the ground forces. The Sabers continued to expand their limits and trained in warfighting functions with sound doctrinal knowledge, which enhanced their overall readiness for the mission in Korea.

In May, 5-17 ACS executed Operation Saber Slash, a movement-to-contact mission against a live opposing force. During this operation, the Sabers enhanced their wartime readiness through various activities, including platoon operations, mobile refueling and rearming, long-distance command and control, extensive use of unmanned aircraft systems (UASs), and training for their downed aircraft recovery team.

In July, 5-17 ACS executed Operation Shield, which focused on expeditionary deployment operations. Saber Squadron increased combat readiness by conducting numerous reconnaissance missions, mobile aircraft refuel/rearm, long-range command and control, downed aircraft recovery training, and the integration of its UAS drones throughout the operation.

The troopers of the 5-17 ACS have conducted three Spur Rides during the 2024-2025 period. Upholding the time-honored tradition of the cavalry trooper, the Sabers extended an invitation to any "Shavetail" brave enough to participate in the journey to earn the coveted Silver Spur. From May 2024 to May 2025, an impressive total of 445 Shavetails rose to the challenge and participated in the Spur Rides.

The 5th of the 17th Air Cavalry Squadron stands ready to meet the challenge: **Out Front, In Support!**

Cav Hat in Saber Apache Gunship Flying Near Korean DMZ
Photo Courtesy of 2nd Infantry Division Public Affairs

Cav Hats, Sabers, Spurs, and Snow
5-17 ACS Command Team – Spur Ride, November 2024
Photo Courtesy of 2nd Infantry Division Public Affairs

Saber & ROK Troopers Enjoy Post-Spur Ride BBQ
Photo Courtesy of 2nd Infantry Division Public Affairs

7th Squadron, 17th Cavalry Regiment

The 7th Squadron, 17th Cavalry Regiment was formally reactivated for training on November 25, 1966, and shortly thereafter adopted the name "Ruthless Riders." The squadron arrived in Vietnam on October 28, 1967, operating as a separate air cavalry squadron tasked with providing reconnaissance and security for the 4th Infantry Division and other allied units. It routinely conducted aggressive combat operations, gathered valuable intelligence, and boldly engaged the enemy, resulting in numerous kills and captures. For its distinguished combat service, the squadron was awarded a Presidential Unit Citation and four Valorous Unit Awards.

Palehorse

Years later, the 7th of the 17th Cavalry Squadron proudly assumed the nickname "Palehorse." Then, on October 22, 2015, the 7th of the 17th Cavalry Squadron was reconstituted as part of the 1st Air Cavalry Brigade, 1st Cavalry Division, at Fort Hood, Texas. This newly configured unit became a Heavy Attack Reconnaissance Squadron, comprised of both AH-64E Apache helicopters and Shadow v2 unmanned aircraft system aircraft.

From January to May 2018, the squadron was deployed to Syria and Iraq, playing a crucial role in support of CENTCOM (U.S. Central Command covering Northeast Africa to Central and South Asia). During this pivotal deployment, Chief Warrant

Officer 3 Jude Okpala and Chief Warrant Officer 5 Steven Crandall were awarded the Distinguished Flying Cross for their extraordinary heroism. On February 7, 2018, the courageous aerial combat of Okpala and Crandall in the AH-64 Apache Attack Helicopter prevented ISIS from overrunning several U.S. positions. Their actions were instrumental in the success of the Special Operations Joint Task Force during the intense "Battle of Conoco Oilfield," situated east of Dayr az-Zawr, Syria.

In late 2019, after a stint at the National Training Center, the 7th of the 17th deployed to Korea and assumed the duties of the Rotational Aviation Force. Returning to Fort Hood, Texas, the Palehorse Squadron participated in gunnery training and testing of experimental equipment before redeploying to Korea in September 2020.

In December 2021, the 7th of the 17th was called to support EUCOM in Eastern Europe in response to heightened tensions against NATO allies. During this operation, the unit was split between Greece and Germany. Midway through the rotation, operational changes required relocating all 7th of the 17th elements to Powidz Airbase in Poland. This move was in response to the Russian invasion of Ukraine and to support and reinforce our Polish NATO allies.

From Poland, the 7th of the 17th executed a critical gap crossing into Lativa, learning valuable lessons for future survivability. Critical training during this rotation included two Joint Multinational Readiness Center training cycles in Germany and a Squadron Gunnery in Poland. Palehorse Squadron returned to Fort Hood in September 2022.

RECENT YEARS

In 2023, the 7-17 Squadron embraced new opportunities by testing a fresh DIVCAV concept for the 1st Cavalry Division in preparation for a rotation at the National Training Center. Throughout the remainder of the year, the squadron concentrated on gunnery tasks and prepared for its EUCOM rotation in 2024. As part of the Army's unmanned aircraft systems (UAS) modernization effort, the squadron also divested itself of the RQ-7B Shadow.

In May 2024, the 7th of the 17th Air Cavalry Squadron was officially organized into Task Force Palehorse as it deployed to Powidz Airbase in Poland. This Task Force included an attachment of MQ-1C Gray Eagle unmanned aircraft systems and UH-60L Black Hawk helicopters. During this rotation, Task Force Palehorse actively participated in several NATO operations, including Iron Wolf in Latvia and Operation Spartan Dagger in Germany.

Palehorse Operations

In recent years, the 7th of the 17th Air Cavalry Squadron has been diligently engaged in critical deployments, rigorous training operations, and rotational assignments. Palehorse Squadron, based out of Fort Hood, Texas, has a proud tradition of worldwide deployment to conduct reconnaissance and security operations to locate and identify enemy forces and destroy those forces when called upon while operating in support of our allied countries.

LTC Ben McDaniel, Commander, 7th of the 17th Cavalry
Welcomes French Soldiers to an Aviation Capabilities Visit
At Forward Operating Site Powidz in Poland, July 17, 2024
Photo by PFC Julian Winston *DVIDS

Palehorse Spur Ride in Poland – October 26, 2024
(l to r) CPT Benjamin Gochee, CW2 Kyle Davidson,
CW2 Peadar Seoighe, CW2 Steven Morris
Photo Courtesy of CW2 Steven Morris

CW2 Ryan May, Bravo Troop, 7-17 Air Cavalry
Stands next to Scalp Hunter Insignia on Apache Gunship
First Local Flight as Pilot in Command
Powidz, Poland, November 1922
Photo Courtesy of 1SG Espinel

1ST SQUADRON, 6TH CAVALRY REGIMENT

The Sixth Cavalry Regiment was established on August 24, 1861, in preparation for the Civil War. During the war, the brave troopers of The Fighting Sixth fought on horseback throughout the Peninsula Campaign and participated in several significant battles, including Mechanicsville, Antietam, Fredericksburg, Gettysburg, Cold Harbor, and Appomattox.

Following the Civil War, The Fighting Sixth served on the prairies of the western frontier, notably in Kansas, Colorado, and Texas. Their mission was to track down and capture Geronimo and his Apache warriors. Ironically, The Fighting Sixth's airframe is now represented by the Apache attack helicopter, which is named in honor of the brave Native American warriors that the 6th Cavalry once fought against.

BATTLES AND DISTINGUISHED TROOPERS

During World War II, The Fighting Sixth maintained its proud heritage, participating in key battles from Normandy to the Battle of the Bulge and ultimately to Berlin as a mechanized cavalry unit. Some of America's finest troopers have served with The Fighting Sixth, including its most distinguished trooper, General John J. Pershing, who was a lieutenant in the squadron during the Boxer Rebellion.

PRESENT-DAY CAVALRY

After multiple activations and deactivations, the 6th Cavalry Regiment completely transformed from the "horse soldiers" of the past into the modern air cavalry squadron we see today. On January 17, 1985, the 1st Squadron was reactivated as one of the pioneer AH-64 Apache units, known as an Armor Attack Helicopter squadron. In this role, the squadron served as a leader in doctrine development and validation for the AH-64 Apache.

The Fighting Sixth, based in Fort Riley, Kansas, deployed to Kuwait in February 2003 in support of Operation Iraqi Freedom. A few years later, in 2005, the 1st Squadron, along with its sister unit, the 2nd Squadron, deployed to Afghanistan. There, they combined with elements from other units to form Task Force Saber.

On June 30, 2006, The Fighting Sixth was reactivated as an air cavalry reconnaissance squadron, equipped with thirty OH-58D Kiowa Warrior helicopters. For the first time in nearly a century, The Fighting Sixth returned to the Mexican border, patrolling from Fort Bliss, Texas, to Playas, New Mexico, in cooperation with the U.S. Customs and Border Protection.

The squadron then deployed to Iraq in support of Operation Iraqi Freedom and redeployed to Fort Carson, Colorado in October 2008.

In 2009, the squadron relocated to its new home on the prairie of Fort Riley, Kansas, following the Army's establishment of the 1st Combat Aviation Brigade. Then, in 2010, The Fighting Sixth returned to Iraq to support Operation Iraqi Freedom and Operation New Dawn. The squadron's troopers were deployed across Iraq, with the Six-Shooter Headquarters Troop stationed in Mosul, Avenger Troop in Taji, and Crusader Troop in Kirkuk, all supporting ground forces. The Fighting Sixth upheld its long tradition of excellence, earning a Meritorious Unit Citation upon redeployment to Fort Riley.

In 2013, The Fighting Sixth continued its support in the Global War on Terror by deploying to Kandahar, Afghanistan, to support Operation Enduring Freedom.

In June 2015, the OH-58D Kiowa Warrior conducted its final flight, and The Fighting Sixth transitioned to a heavy attack reconnaissance squadron, embracing the advanced capabilities and formidable firepower of the AH-64E Apache gunship.

In support of Operation Atlantic Resolve, The Fighting Sixth completed a rotation to Powidz, Poland, in 2023.

The Fighting Sixth has undergone significant evolution over the regiment's proud history, transitioning from horseback to aircraft. However, the mission of the cavalry remains the same: to provide essential reconnaissance and engage America's adversaries to secure victory in our nation's wars.

LTC Jonathan Ryder Accepts Colors from COL Chad Corrigan
Change of Command Ceremony, Powidz, Poland, May 2024
Photo by Captain Jordan Beagle *DVIDS

LTC John McLean – CO, 1st of the 6th Cavalry
Addresses the Squadron at Change of Command Ceremony
Fort Riley, Kansas, Cavalry Parade Field, June 9, 2022
Photo Courtesy PFC Dawson Smith *DVIDS

1st of the 6th Cavalry – Pass in Review
Change of Command Ceremony, Fort Riley, KS, June 6, 2022
Photo Courtesy of PFC Dawson Smith *DVIDS

2ND SQUADRON, 6TH CAVALRY REGIMENT

The 6th Cavalry Regiment was constituted on May 4, 1861, and organized at Camp Scott in Pennsylvania. The regiment fought valiantly in the Civil War as part of the Union's first action in the Peninsula Campaign on May 4, 1862. In recognition of its distinguished service as a key component of the Union Army of the Potomac, the unit earned sixteen battle streamers.

It was during the Gettysburg Campaign in 1863, at Williamsburg, Pennsylvania, that the regiment received its Coat of Arms distinction, and the first member of the regiment earned the Medal of Honor. Against overwhelming odds and relentless assaults from superior Confederate cavalry forces, the 6th Cavalry Regiment stood firm and demonstrated exceptional resilience. Their decisive actions successfully disrupted a formidable contingent of elite cavalry troopers from General Jeb Stuart's command. Despite sustaining heavy casualties, the regiment's fighting spirit and determination to persist earned them the Unicorn, shown rampant on the Coat of Arms, symbolizing their knightly virtues.

Following the Civil War, the 6th Cavalry left Maryland for Austin, Texas, in 1865 to be a part of the 5th Military District, which encompassed Texas and Louisiana. During the majority of the 1870s and 1880s, the 6th Cavalry was based in the Southwest and served in the thick of the Apache Campaigns. The 6th Cavalry participated in ten Indian Campaigns and was responsible for the surrender of the famous Apache chief Geronimo.

THE 2ND OF THE 6TH CAVALRY TODAY

Stationed in Hawaii, the 2nd of the 6th Air Cavalry Squadron plays a vital role in United States operations across the Indo-Pacific region. As the only forward-postured attack helicopter squadron in the Pacific, it is a key player in regional deterrence and joint force integration.

The squadron trains and operates alongside units from the U.S. Marine Corps, Navy, Air Force, and Special Operations. It also maintains strong partnerships with allies, particularly in the Philippines.

The 2nd of the 6th also trains regularly with the 25th Air Support Operations Squadron to maintain Close Air Support proficiency. Through these efforts, the squadron continues to enhance its readiness and strengthen regional partnerships.

AERIAL GUNNERY

The 2nd of the 6th Air Cavalry Squadron conducts aerial gunnery live-fire training at Pohakuloa Training Area (PTA) on the Big Island of Hawaii. Located between the volcanic peaks of Mauna Kea and Mauna Loa, PTA is the Army's premier live-fire and combined arms training center in the Pacific. Its rugged landscape, covered in hardened lava rock and roamed by wild goats, provides a challenging and realistic environment for aviation training.

The squadron occupies PTA for up to a month, beginning with crew qualifications on the .50-caliber machine gun and MK19 grenade launcher. These exercises then progress into full aerial gunnery tables. Crews fly by day and night, executing team-based qualification missions, firing 30mm cannon rounds, point-detonating rockets, and flechettes at targets across the range.

Transformation to the AH-64E Version 6

In early 2024, the 2nd of the 6th Air Cavalry Squadron fielded twenty-one new AH-64E Version 6 Guardian attack helicopters. This modernization effort replaced the aging AH-64D Longbow fleet. With the fielding completed in 2025, Renegade, Shock, and Chaos Troops now operate the most advanced attack helicopters in the Army inventory.

This transformation is the latest in a long line of evolutions for the cavalry. From the horse-mounted troopers of the past to the OH-58D Kiowa Warrior, to the AH-64D Longbow, and now the AH-64E Version 6, the cavalry's platform may change, but its mission and legacy endure.

Additionally, the squadron continues to integrate modernized unmanned aircraft systems (UAS) into its formations. Small UAS platforms are being fielded and employed to enhance intelligence, surveillance, and reconnaissance capabilities. These systems support Apache operations by extending situational awareness and increasing the effectiveness of reconnaissance and movement-to-contact missions.

The Spur Ride

The Spur Ride is a longstanding cavalry tradition that welcomes new soldiers, known as "Shavetails," into the formation. Its purpose is to challenge troopers mentally and physically, testing their strength, tactical proficiency, and mental agility. Those who complete the events face a final assessment before a Spur Board composed of senior leaders.

The 2nd of the 6th Air Cavalry Squadron conducts this rite of passage on the island of Oahu, navigating the rugged terrain of Makua Valley and Dillingham Airfield. During the event, troopers ruck fifteen miles through jungles and mountains while learning about the legacy of the cavalry, the history of their unit, and the significance of the land they traverse.

The Spur Ride culminates on a sunlit beach where Shavetails line up beside their fellow troopers. At the Senior Spur Holder's command, they charge into the cold ocean surf. There, Spur Holders put them through pushups in the sand and waves. In a moment that symbolizes both exhaustion and pride, each Shavetail receives their silver spurs, fastened to their boots by their sponsor or a Spur Holder. This moment represents their connection to the cavalry and to those who came before them. Traditions like these enrich the legacy of the cavalry and make Hawaii a meaningful home for the 2nd of the 6th Air Cavalry Squadron and the U.S. Army.

THE STETSON IN THE MODERN ERA

For modern cavalry troopers in the 2nd of the 6th Air Cavalry Squadron, the black Stetson remains a meaningful symbol of pride, tradition, and accomplishment. Troopers often receive their Stetson after completing gunnery, surviving a tough field rotation, or stepping into a leadership role. Unit events, like the "Stetson Break-in," honor this tradition.

Even in a digital age marked by advanced technology and modern warfare, the Stetson continues to connect troopers to generations past. Whether supporting joint operations, deploying across the Pacific, or flying the Army's most lethal helicopters, troopers still earn their spurs and wear the Stetson with pride – knowing they are part of a proud and enduring legacy.

2nd of the 6th Cavalry, Change of Command Ceremony
Wheeler Army Airfield, Hawaii, May 28, 2025
Photo by SPC Charles Clark *DVIDS

LTC Matthew R. Clawson Addresses the Formation
Change of Command Ceremony, May 28, 2025
Photo by SPC Charles Clark, *DVIDS

4th Squadron, 6th Cavalry Regiment

Established in August 1861 in response to the need for an additional cavalry regiment during the Civil War, the 6th Cavalry emerged from the strategic restructuring of the 3rd Cavalry. In March 1862, the regiment took to the field in Virginia, playing an integral role within the Army of the Potomac.

The 6th Cavalry Regiment served in sixteen campaigns, engaging in frequent bitter and bloody battles, among them Antietam, Gettysburg, the Wilderness Campaign, and Appomattox.

Indian Wars

After the Civil War, the 6th Cavalry was deployed to the West, where it spent over thirty years policing the frontier and engaging in numerous skirmishes with Native American tribes. By the end of the regiment's service in the West, the 6th Cavalry had fought against many hostile tribes, including the Comanche and Apache, and was credited with participation in ten Indian War Campaigns.

Overseas Campaigns

In 1898, the 6th Cavalry Regiment sailed to Cuba, where it took part in the assault on San Juan Hill alongside the "Rough Riders" of the 1st U.S. Volunteer Cavalry. The regiment then embarked on a vital mission to China in 1900 as part of a relief expedition, returning triumphantly to the United States in 1903. In 1907, the regiment firmly established its presence in the Philippines. In 1909, the 6th Cavalry decisively defeated the Moros in a significant battle on Jolo, showcasing its prowess and resilience.

The following year the regiment sailed for France, serving in the rear echelon during World War I. Upon its return from France in 1919, the 6th Cavalry went to Fort Oglethorpe, Georgia, where it resided for the next twenty-three years.

Present Day

In February 2019, the 4th of the 6th Air Cavalry, designated a Heavy Attack Reconnaissance Squadron, stationed at Joint Base Lewis-McChord in Washington, deployed to Camp Humphreys in the Republic of Korea. This deployment supported the United States Army Pacific (USARPAC) and the Indo-Pacific Unified Combatant Command (INDOPACOM), with the mission of deterring aggression from the Democratic People's Republic of Korea (DPRK).

The squadron returned to its home base at Joint Base Lewis-McChord in October 2019, leaving its twenty-four AH-64 Apache helicopters in the Republic of Korea to ensure a smooth transition for rotational forces in the region. Upon their return, the 4th of the 6th Air Cavalry fielded twenty-four AH-64 Apache gunships from the 7th of the 17th Air Cavalry Squadron, 1st Cavalry Division Combat Aviation Brigade, at Fort Hood, Texas.

Deployment to Korea Again

Throughout most of 2020, the 4th of the 6th Air Cavalry Squadron rotated through several cycles of gunnery training at the Yakima Training Center, Washington. Then, in the summer of 2021, the squadron transferred all twenty-four Apache gunships to the 1st of the 6th Air Cavalry Squadron based at Fort Riley, Kansas.

In September 2021, the 4th of the 6th Squadron deployed again to the Republic of Korea, this time utilizing the Apache gunships left in Korea from their previous deployment. This deployment lasted nine months, after which the squadron redeployed to Joint Base Lewis-McChord in June 2022. There, they fielded twenty-one AH-64 helicopters from the 2nd of the 17th Air Cavalry Squadron at Fort Campbell and two Apache gunships previously transferred to the 1st of the 6th Cavalry.

NATIONAL TRAINING CENTER

In April and May 2024, the 4th of the 6th Air Cavalry Squadron served as the Aviation Task Force headquarters at the National Training Center, supporting the 1st of the 2nd Stryker Brigade Combat Team.

SPUR RIDE

A Spur Ride was held in July 2024, to train Squadron troopers on cavalry fundamentals, appreciate its history, and build esprit de corps. During this event, ninety-five Shavetails were awarded their silver spurs.

CURRENT OPERATIONS

After another Spur Ride in June 2025 where eighty-one Shavetails earned their silver spurs, the squadron executed a Field Training Exercise at Joint Base Lewis-McChord and Naval Air Station North Island, California, to demonstrate capabilities for operations in the INDOPACOM region, focusing on command and control beyond line of sight and improving lethality.

In September 2025, B Troop will participate in Super Garuda Shield 2025 exercises in Indonesia to provide assurance to INDOPACOM allies and partners.

4th of 6th Cav Hat and Spurs
Belonging to LTC Jay Berger
Photo Courtesy of CW3 Chris Cannaday

4-6 Cavalry Command Group, Yakima Training Center, WA, 2024
(l to r) LTC Jay Berger, CSM Les Underwood, CW4 Randy Turner,
MAJ Dan Prior, and MAJ Sharon Wheelock
Photo Courtesy of Captain Bryce Gandy

Apache Maintenance & Cleaning, Yuma, AZ, August 2022
(l to r) CPT Brett Hamilton and CW3 John McIlwain
Photo Courtesy of CW2 Jenson Bartlett

6th Squadron, 6th Cavalry Regiment

On the sixth day of the sixth month in 1990, the 6th Squadron of the 6th U.S. Cavalry Regiment was reactivated at Fort Hood, Texas. The squadron was tasked with training on the new AH-64A Apache attack helicopter platform. It fielded twenty-four Apaches, designating them as "Combat Ready," which meant they had the aerial combat power and soldier readiness to defeat an enemy tank division. Equipped and trained to excel in combat, the 6th Squadron deployed to Germany to establish a combat-ready presence in the region.

Early Iraq

In 1991, during the persecution of the Kurdish people instigated by Saddam Hussein, the 6th Squadron deployed to northern Iraq within ninety-six hours. Their swift action and ominous presence in the region provided relief to the Kurdish people, enabling their return home.

Bosnia and Kosovo

Throughout the 1990s, the squadron actively engaged in peacekeeping operations in Bosnia and Kosovo. In 2001, the squadron returned to Fort Hood, Texas, to transition to the AH-64D Longbow Apache, becoming the first unit in U.S. Army Europe (USAREUR) to implement this upgraded platform.

After a year of training, they redeployed to Illesheim, Germany, in 2002.

OPERATION IRAQI FREEDOM

Initially, there were rumors about a deployment to Kuwait in late 2002; however, the squadron ultimately deployed to Iraq in March 2003 as part of Operation Iraqi Freedom, where they remained until March 2004.

On January 23, 2007, as part of the Army's modular transformation, the 6-6 Cavalry Squadron was reflagged and reactivated as an OH-58D Kiowa Warrior Squadron under the 10th Mountain Division, 10th Combat Aviation Brigade at Fort Drum, New York. Then, in 2008, the unit deployed to Iraq again, where they formed a unique dual-airframe squadron that combined OH-58Ds and AH-64Ds.

OPERATION ENDURING FREEDOM XI

In 2010, Task Force Six Shooters was deployed to Afghanistan for Operation Enduring Freedom XI. During their deployment, they accumulated over 30,000 flight hours and took part in 140 aerial reconnaissance operations. The task force received multiple valor awards, including Distinguished Flying Crosses, and was recognized as the AAAA Outstanding Aviation Unit of the Year.

HEAVY ATTACK RECONNAISSANCE SQUADRON

In 2011, the unit returned to Fort Drum and remained task-organized until 2014. After troop reintegration, the squadron focused on training and began divesting the OH-58D Kiowa helicopters. In 2015, they deployed to Korea as a rotational unit. The squadron returned to Fort Drum in August 2016 and transitioned into a Heavy Attack Reconnaissance Squadron (H-ARS), incorporating both AH-64D Apache helicopters and RQ-7B Shadow unmanned aerial vehicles (UAVs).

Freedom's Sentinel and Resolute Support

The squadron maintained a high operational tempo throughout the late 2010s and early 2020s. It deployed to Korea again in 2017, supporting regional deterrence efforts amid rising tensions with North Korea. After returning to Fort Drum in 2018, the unit deployed to Afghanistan in 2019 for Operations Freedom's Sentinel and Resolute Support.

Recent Years

Stationed at Fort Drum, New York, the squadron began a proof-of-concept in 2022 to integrate its RQ-7B Shadow drones into a standalone unmanned aircraft system (UAS) detachment. This initiative demonstrates the squadron's ongoing adaptation to modern combat requirements and its commitment to operational excellence.

In 2025, the squadron focused on developing leaders and pilots who were prepared for Large-Scale Combat Operations (LSCO) through rigorous Division Warfighter exercises and a renewed emphasis on historical cavalry traditions.

Recognizing its upcoming inactivation in December 2025, the Six Shooters held their final Spur Ride in June. This culminating event, deeply rooted in the squadron's proud history, was designed to test trooper skills and bolster esprit de corps while also serving as a poignant celebration of the unit's distinguished legacy and ongoing contributions to Army Aviation.

Mountain Fest Streamer on D Troop Guidon
SFC Shelly Bamburg and 2LT Victoria VanMeter
Fort Drum, NY, June 26, 2025
Photo by SPC Mariah Aguilar *DVIDS

Captain Dennis Howard
Ruck March During Spur Ride, May 6, 2024
Fort Drum, New York
Photo by Sergeant Jamie Robinson *DVIDS

CHAPTER 9
HORSE CAVALRY DETACHMENT

In telling the story of the Cav Hat, the horse detachments of the United States Army provide a rare glimpse of the campaign hat and uniforms worn by mounted cavalry troopers in the late 1800s. The most widely recognized of those detachments is that of the 1st Cavalry Division.

1ST CAVALRY DIVISION HORSE DETACHMENT

The Horse Cavalry Detachment of the 1st Cavalry Division, located at Fort Hood, Texas, was established in 1972 under the leadership of Major General James C. Smith, the commander of the 1st Cavalry Division. General Smith was recognized for his ability to boost morale among his troops as well as his strong public relations skills. As one of only five mounted cavalry units currently active in the United States Army, the 1st Cavalry Division Detachment embodies the spirit of the United States Cavalry and honors the proud heritage of the 1st Cavalry Division.

It has been over eighty years since the last mounted troopers of the 1st Cavalry Division traded their horses for jeeps, trucks, and tanks in preparation for their deployment in World War II to fight the Japanese in the Pacific Theater. Although the era of mounted troops and squadrons is behind us, the spirit and traditions of the old cavalry are vividly brought to life by the 1st Cavalry Division Horse Detachment.

1870S UNIFORMS AND HORSE TACK

The Horse Detachment garrison, workshops, and stables are situated in a rural area next to the main entrance of Fort Hood. This detachment is organized and equipped to represent the division as a 1870s-era "horse soldier" troop. The soldiers wear cavalry uniforms that consist of government-issued blouses, trousers, belts, boots, and Cav Hats modeled off the 1876 campaign hats. They are also armed with authentic firearms, sabers, saddles, and period-appropriate work details.

The standard weapons provided to the troops include the 1873 Model 45-70 Springfield "Trap Door" Carbine, the 1873 Colt Single Action .45-caliber revolver, and the 1860 Light Cavalry Saber, which was standard issue during the Civil War. The horses are equipped with McClellan 1885 Saddles, which have been modified with the 1904 quarter strap.

The close-order mounted drills are patterned as in the 1883 Manual of Cavalry Tactics. Even the horses chosen for platoon mounts are selected to the same physical standards imposed a century ago. Each horse must be no less than fifteen hands high, and it must be dark, with a minimum of white markings. In addition to the horses and mules, the platoon has a restored Studebaker escort wagon from the 1890s. The wagon was originally used to haul supplies, but it is now mainly used in Horse Detachment ceremonies and demonstrations.

HORSE DETACHMENT TROOPERS

When not engaged in ceremonial or parade duty, the troopers are assigned garrison duties that reflect the era they represent. In addition to their regular military training, troopers in the detachment are responsible for grooming, feeding, and caring for their horses. They also maintain all tack equipment and receive training in weapons and saddle restoration, boot making, and horseshoeing.

A significant aspect of horse care involves paying close attention to the horses' hooves. Approximately every four to six weeks, the iron horseshoes need to be replaced. Proper selection, use, and fitting of horseshoes provide essential benefits, including: protection and support for the horses' hooves, correction of hoof conformation issues, prevention of uneven hoof wear, maintenance of proper hoof form and balance, and improvement in the distribution of the horse's weight across the hoof.

Self-Sustaining Detachment

The detachment functions as a self-sufficient unit, providing all necessary specialized functional support. The leather shop is equipped with the hand tools and specialized machinery required for tack repair and remanufacturing, saddle repair and restoration, and boot repair and manufacturing. This equipment is primarily utilized during the late fall and winter months to ensure that all gear is ready for the spring and summer parade season.

In addition to maintaining their personal gear, each trooper also oversees a small "motor pool" that includes special horse trailers used for transporting horses to remote locations, as well as equipment trailers.

The detachment consists of forty troopers, forty-seven horses, eight mules, an M-1878 supply wagon, and an M-1841 light mountain howitzer cannon.

Performances

Since its establishment in 1972, the detachment has performed for a wide range of audiences, including prestigious events such as presidential inaugural parades, the 1984 World's Fair, the annual Tournament of Roses Parade, and thousands of state and local fairs, parades, and rodeos. The detachment showcases both formal military parades and reviews, as well as civic and community street parades. Additionally, it features a thirty-minute mounted drill and weapons demonstration.

The mounted demonstration is an exciting exhibition of the skill and precision required of each mounted trooper. It includes drill maneuvers performed at the walk, trot, and canter. The weapons portion of the show highlights the mounted use of the cavalry saber, the Colt .45-caliber revolver, and the Springfield Carbine.[25]

HORSE DETACHMENT PHASE-OUT

In July 2025, the Army announced plans to drop most of its horses, mules, and donkeys over the next year. In a news release, the Office of the Assistant Secretary of the Army Manpower and Reserve Affairs explained that it would "sunset ownership, operation and materiel support" of its Military Working Equid programs "to align more resources with warfighting capability and readiness."

Thus, the 1st Cavalry Division Horse Detachment will fade into the sunset. "Once we receive the official order, we will have one year to seamlessly transition our equids to responsible owners, prioritizing their welfare and maintaining the highest standards of care during this process," 1st Cavalry Major Tevin Radford said. "The 1st Cavalry Division Horse Detachment has been a proud symbol of the division's heritage for over fifty-three years, playing a vital role in community relations and representing the division and the Army with distinction at national events, including the Army's 250th birthday parade. The 1st Cavalry Division remains committed to its mission of

---

[25] "History of the 1st Cavalry Division Horse Detachment." The 1st Cavalry Division Association website. https://1cda.org/history/history-1cd-horse-det/.

warfighting, readiness and service to the nation, while honoring the legacy of our horse detachment."[26]

SPC Gwendolyne Grosscup and Her Horse Zeus
Pose in the Horse Detachment Barn, Dec. 6, 2024
Photo by Scott Darling *DVIDS

---

[26] Writer, Brent Johnson | Herald Staff. 2025. "Army to Phase Out 1st Cav Horse Detachment, Other Equine Units." *Killeen Daily Herald*. July 8, 2025. https://kdhnews.com/fort_hood_herald/army-to-phase-out-1st-cav-horse-detachment-other-equine-units/article_a36524c4-501d-47c9-96f1-75f2ec00b043.html#google_vignette.

Captain Daysha Wells, Horse Detachment Commander
Army's 250th Birthday Parade in Washington, D.C.
June 14, 2025
Photo by Specialist David Dumas *DVIDS

The Horse Cavalry Detachment, led by First Sergeant Kyle Minor,
Presents Arms during the National Anthem.
Photo Courtesy of 1st Cavalry Division PAO

Charge onto Cooper Field – SSG Rivas and SGT Luna, June 3, 2025
Mule Team, Trudy and Traveler
Photo Courtesy of 1st Cavalry Division PAO

SPC Donovin Allen Riding Nobody, May 17, 2024
Change of Command flower presentation on Cooper Field
Photo Courtesy of 1st Cavalry Division PAO

Horse Detachment's M1841 Light Mountain Howitzer
Photo Courtesy of 1st Cavalry Division PAO

SSG Jason Bishop, Horse Detachment Military Trainer
National Cavalry Competition in El Reno, OK, 2016
Photo by Sergeant Marcus Floyd *DVIDS

CHAPTER 10
CAV HAT CREASES AND BRIMS

Once cavalry troopers acquire their Cav Hats, they face two important decisions: 1) how to shape the brim, and 2) how to form the crown, commonly known as the crease. This chapter presents various examples of cavalry hat creases and brim styles. However, before we explore these options, let's take a brief look at the story behind hat creases.

HISTORY OF THE CREASE

To understand how hat shapes evolved over the years, we once again turn to Stetson. The original "Boss of the Plains" design featured a flat brim and a rounded crown. This style dominated for about twenty years, and many nineteenth-century photographs reveal that these hats generally did not have a deliberate crease; instead, most were kept with an open crown.

But, through use, abuse, and customization by individual wearers, hats were modified from their original appearance. Notably, the crown would become dented, at first inadvertently, then by deliberate choice of individual owners.

Over time, hat styles began to evolve. One of the earliest popular modifications was the introduction of a long crease that sloped from the high back down toward the front, known as the "Carlsbad crease." Another notable design that emerged in this era was the "Montana peak," characterized by its four distinctive dents around the crown. This unique feature originated from the way the hat was handled on top with four fingers.

The brim of the hat was frequently rolled or curved, with unique ornamentation added to reflect personal style. These creases and brim shapes often reflected the owner's location or occupation. In some instances, individual cowboys could be identified by the distinctive crease in their hats, which signified the ranch where they worked. Similarly, the cavalry hat brim and crease often reflected the trooper's unit.

In the early days, nearly every Stetson hat was shipped with an open crown, leaving it to skilled hat shops to shape the crown and brims. The original creases soon became known as the five "Stetson" creases, as illustrated in the following Stetson display.[27]

The Five Famous Stetson Creases

---

[27] Correa, Tom. n.d. "John B. Stetson – 'Father of the Cowboy Hat.'" http://www.americancowboychronicles.com/2015/12/john-b-stetson-father-of-cowboy-hat.html.

Cav Hat Creases

The cavalry hat, as supplied by Stetson, featured a wide, single crease running from front to back. The brim was flat, with a slight upturn around its edge. Some troopers chose to wear their hats "as is" with no modifications, but most elected to make some refinements to the crown, brim, or both.

Stetson Crease

During the Vietnam War, there were no facilities where soldiers could have their cavalry hats steamed and shaped. As a result, many cavalry troopers wore their hats straight out of the box from Stetson, maintaining the single Stetson crease. The only modification was to flatten the brim and create a slight downward pitch on all sides. A notable example of this common hat style is George Abernathy's hat displayed later in "Cav Hat Brims."

Stetson Cavalry Hat
Photo Courtesy of CavHooah

The Cavalry Pinch

One of the most popular styles of Cav Hats during the Vietnam War combines the classic Stetson Crease with a distinctive "pinch" on each side of the crown. In the accompanying photos, you can clearly see this pinch, as well as the "Cavalry Slouch" brim described later in this chapter.

The Cavalry Pinch with Cavalry Slouch Brim
Photo of John Edmunds at 2025 VHPA reunion

THE "PORK PIE" CREASE

The "Pork Pie" crease was popular among several cavalry troops during the Vietnam War, particularly the "Stogie Scouts" of B Troop, 3rd of the 17th Air Cavalry. This trend may have been influenced by the TV show *Wanted Dead or Alive*, which starred Steve McQueen, known for wearing a Stetson with a pork pie crown. Said to resemble the British pastry meat pie, pork pie hats were common in mid-nineteenth-century England.

This "stovepipe" shaped hat is also called the "Telescope" crease by today's western wear hat shops. The hats shown below were worn by cavalry troopers during the Vietnam War.

Stogie Scout Cav Hat
B Troop, 3rd of the 17th Cav

Rick Schwab's Cav Hat
C Troop, 2nd of the 17th Cav

THE PINCH FRONT CREASE

The Pinch Front crease is a modification of the pork pie crease with two front pinches that compress the circular crown into a teardrop shape. This hat style gained popularity after John Wayne wore several variations of it in the iconic cavalry movies produced by John Ford in the late 1940s and early 1950s. The silverbelly Cav Hat below features the pinch front crease and rolled brim.

Lighthorse Silverbelly Cavalry Hat
With Pinch Front Crease and Rolled Brim

THE CAVALRY CATTLEMAN CREASE

The Cavalry Cattleman Crease boasts a storied history that dates back more than a century. Notably, this iconic hat style was worn by Trooper Adolphus McGill of the 11th Cavalry Regiment in 1906, as shown earlier in this book.

The Cattleman crease is the most traditional crease for cowboy hats and is defined by three creases running from front to back, with the center crease being the longest. In the cavalry variation, the center crease is narrower, and the side creases are often referred to as "dents." The Cavalry Cattleman crease continues to be popular among today's cavalry troops.

Cavalry Cattleman Crease
CPT Larry Glover, HHT, 3-17 Air Cavalry Squadron

The Cavalry "Gus" Crease

This Cavalry "Gus" crease is a variation of the "Gus" cowboy hat that gained popularity in the 1990s. Named after Augustus McCrae from the miniseries *Lonesome Dove*, the hat features a high crown at the back that slopes downward toward the front. It often includes a front "pinch" on both sides of the crown

The Cavalry "Gus" Crease
1LT Hayden Moelter, C/3-17 Air Cavalry

THE BLACKHORSE CREASE

The brown campaign hat was developed in 2002 when Greeley Hat Works was asked to design and produce the Blackhorse campaign hats to resemble the 1883 style campaign hat worn by 11th Cavalry troopers in the early 1900s.

To design this hat, Trent Johnson, a skilled hatmaker and owner of Greeley Hat Works, sought inspiration from the Blackhorse Museum at Fort Irvin, California. There, he meticulously studied an early 1900s campaign hat on display. Drawing from the rich history of this prototype, Trent crafted the modern Blackhorse campaign hat.

The "Blackhorse Crease," is a variation of the traditional cattleman crease. What sets this crease apart is a distinctive "mule kick" dent at the front crown. According to Trent, this unique feature originated from cavalry troopers who would push their soft felt hats down securely onto their heads while riding.

The hat color was inspired by historical photos of early 1900s campaign hats worn by the 11th Cavalry, Teddy Roosevelt's Rough Riders, and Roosevelt's own hat. The brim is the classic "Cavalry Slouch" brim, a uniform arc from front to back.

Blackhorse Crease
CSM Vincente Moreno and CPT Jordan Blackman, 11th ACR
Courtesy of Fort Irwin 11th Cavalry Regiment Public Affairs

Cav Hat Brims

Cavalry "Slouch" Brim: The slouch-style brim has emerged as the preferred choice among cavalry troopers. Its distinctive design features a downward curve at both the front and back, creating a smooth arc that enhances both functionality and visual appeal. Several of the preceding hat crease photos have the slouch brim.

Cavalry Rolled Brim: The rolled brim was popular with several cavalry troops in Vietnam. In this style, the side brims are curved upward while maintaining a slight downward curve on the front and rear brims. This brim style was likely influenced by Western movies during that era. The frontal view of the silverbelly hat with a pinch front crease is a good example of the rolled brim style.

Cavalry Flat Brim: The Cavalry Flat brim was created by flattening the new Stetson brim and angling it slightly downward on all sides. George Abernathy's Cav Hat is a good example.

CHAPTER 11
Cav Hat Traditions

"Breaking-In" Ceremony

Cavalry troopers take immense pride in their Cav Hats, viewing them as symbols of honor and tradition. Since the cavalry hat is not issued by the military, it is typically purchased privately, although some may receive their hats as gifts from their troop sponsor or a senior spur holder. However, it is important to note that inductee troopers must refrain from wearing their cavalry hats at unit functions until they have been properly broken in. This tradition underscores the significance and respect associated with the Cav Hat, ensuring that each trooper fully embraces its meaning before wearing the hat publicly.

Connection to History

The breaking-in ceremony of the iconic cavalry hat is not just a tradition; it is a profound ritual deeply rooted in cavalry lore. The custom traces its origins to the late 1800s, during the era of horse-mounted troopers. According to legend, a lone cavalry scout would ingeniously fill the crown of his Army-issued campaign hat with water from his canteen to quench his loyal horse's thirst. Crafted from durable animal fur, the 1883-style campaign hat was not only waterproof but also served as a practical "bucket" for this vital purpose. Embracing this tradition today reinforces the cavalry's connection to the bravery and resourcefulness of the cavalry troopers who came before them.

The legend of the lone cavalry scout watering his horse with his hat is complemented by a 1924 Stetson advertisement that depicted a cowboy giving his horse the last drink from his canteen. In this classic ad, frequently referred to as "The Last Drop," Stetson suggests that their hats are made of such high-quality animal fur that they can hold water, thereby lending credibility to the cavalry legend.[28]

Stetson 1924 Ad
From Lon Megargee Painting

---

[28] Correa, Tom. n.d. "John B. Stetson – 'Father of the Cowboy Hat.'" http://www.americancowboychronicles.com/2015/12/john-b-stetson-father-of-cowboy-hat.html.

TROOP TRADITION

The breaking-in ceremony is a unique tradition that varies among cavalry troops and squadrons, each adding its own distinct character to the event. While the specifics may differ, the essence remains the same: a celebration of tradition and camaraderie. Since the breaking-in ceremony is a non-authorized event, it is held off-post and usually outdoors, depending on the weather.

To be eligible for the cavalry hat breaking-in ceremony, candidate troopers must fulfill one or more of the following criteria. (Please note that qualifications vary by unit.)

- Be in good standing with the troop.
- Have completed a spur ride.
- Returning from deployment.
- Have qualified as Q1 during aerial gunnery.
- Have served with the troop for a specified time.

The ceremony is usually supervised by the commander or senior spur holder, who directs the candidate troopers to assemble in line formation, holding their hats upside down with their spur holder sponsor facing them. The leader then delivers introductory remarks to emphasize the significance of the time-honored tradition, as well as the pride and respect being conferred upon them. As an example, the following introduction was used by Charlie Troop, 3rd of the 17th Cavalry, in their 2015 breaking-in ceremony.

"The tradition of 'breaking in' a cavalry hat is both long-standing and respected. Many troopers believe that a Cav Hat should not be worn unless it has been properly broken in. This custom dates back to the origins of the cavalry, when troopers rode horses and took great care in protecting their steeds. When a trooper arrived at a rocky streambed with steep banks, instead of risking injury to his horse's legs by attempting to climb down, he would collect water from the stream in his cavalry hat, then sample the water himself before allowing his horse to drink from it. Today, we honor that tradition and the history of the 17th Cavalry during this ceremony."

On the command "Pour," the sponsors pour the ritual liquid into the open crown of the hats. The composition of the ritual liquid varies among cavalry units, with beer being the most common ingredient. For those who prefer not to partake in alcohol, a non-alcoholic option is readily available upon request, ensuring that everyone can participate in this proud tradition.

Once the ritual liquid is poured into the Cav Hat, the candidate begins the ceremonial drinking by cautiously tilting the hat upward. After consuming an appropriate amount, the sponsor dramatically slams the Cav Hat onto the candidate's head, totally engulfing the candidate in the ritual liquid. After the soaking, the ceremony concludes when the candidates recite "Fiddler's Green."

Tradition's Origin

This ritual traces its roots back to the Vietnam War and is said to have started with a "newbie" trooper who carelessly set his newly acquired Cav Hat upside down on a table in the officers' club. Seizing the opportunity, one of the more seasoned cavalry troopers filled the open crown of the hat with beer. Not to be outdone, the newbie boldly lifted the hat and used the brim to funnel the beer into his mouth, igniting cheers and laughter from his fellow cavalry troopers. Thus, a tradition was born.

While the veracity of that story remains elusive, it's well documented that around 1968, troopers from the 1st of the 9th, the 7th of the 17th, and other cavalry units engaged in a lively breaking-in ceremony for newbies. During this spirited event, a concoction of various beverages was poured into the open crowns of the newly acquired cavalry hats. The newbies would then drink from their hats, creating a raucous scene as they inevitably spilled a good portion of the mixture. This tradition not only marked their entry into the cavalry but also fostered camaraderie and a sense of belonging among the troopers.

The timing of the ceremony varied among different units. One troop adhered to a guideline that required new members to complete thirty days of service before participating in the ceremony. However, if they "lost their cherry" – meaning their aircraft had sustained hits from hostile fire – this milestone would be recognized earlier. This practice underscored the troop's commitment to honoring time served and the realities of combat.

Today's breaking-in ceremony stands as a tribute to the rich legacy of the Cav Hat, symbolizing not only cavalry pride but also the enduring camaraderie forged among those who serve in the cavalry.

C Troop, 2nd of the 17th Air Cavalry "Breaking In"- December 2022
Photo Courtesy of Captain Megan Kinsey

1LT Larry Glover's Cav Hat "Breaking-In"
Outcasts – C Troop, 6-16 Air Cavalry
Fort Drum, NY – April 2019
Photo Courtesy of Captain Larry Glover

FIDDLER'S GREEN

Halfway down the trail to Hell,
In a shady meadow green
Are the Souls of all dead Troopers camped,
Near a good old-time canteen.
And this eternal resting place
Is known as Fiddler's Green.

Marching past, straight through to Hell
The Infantry are seen.
Accompanied by the Engineers,
Artillery and Marines,
For none but the shades of Cavalrymen
Dismount at Fiddler's Green.

Though some go curving down the trail
To seek a warmer scene.
No Trooper ever gets to Hell
Ere he's emptied his canteen.
And so, rides back to drink again
With friends at Fiddlers' Green.

And so, when man and horse go down
Beneath a saber keen,
Or in a roaring charge of fierce melee,
You stop a bullet clean,
And the hostiles come to get your scalp,
just empty your canteen,
And put your pistol to your head
and go to Fiddler's Green.

Combat Knots

Legend has it that during the age of horse cavalry, the acorns attached to hat cords were designed to bounce off the brim of the campaign hat, a clever tactic to keep riders alert during long journeys. To ensure this functionality, troopers skillfully tied a half-hitch knot on each side of the center slide, often referred to as a "keep." This simple yet effective technique prevented the acorns from dangling off the brim, ensuring the proper "acorn bounce," and thereby enhancing the soldiers' focus and readiness on the move.

In recent years, the knots tied on each side of the "keep" have taken on a new meaning. Known as "Combat Knots," these knots symbolize combat tours. Although there are no official directives or guidelines regarding their usage, the tradition surrounding these knots is deeply respected. Emerging in the years following the Vietnam War, combat knots carry profound significance. Those who wear combat knots do so with pride, signifying their unwavering commitment to our nation and the valor that comes with serving our country in a war zone.

Combat Knots – Half Hitch Close to the Keep

CHAPTER 12
ARMY HUMOR

STETSON – "THE OFFICIAL ARMY HEADGEAR"

On April Fool's Day in 2011, the U.S. Army cleverly published a tongue-in-cheek statement on its website, announcing that the Stetson would become the official headgear for the Army. The following is an excerpt from that announcement.

WASHINGTON, APRIL 1, 2011 – In a fingertip-to-the-brim nod to its American frontier history, the Army is changing hats again – returning to the tumultuous days of the horse cavalry in the wild west and adopting a dark blue Stetson as the official headgear for the current force of 1.1 million Soldiers.

"We figure the Stetson will be popular with the troops," said Sergeant Major Bob S. Stone, Army Uniform Board headgear task force president. "It's been a while since we have changed the headgear, so it's time. Plus, a Stetson is functional and downright American."

But reminiscent of the controversial switch from the garrison cap to the black beret, the Army faces opposition from one community deeply opposed to losing its special identity with the Stetson – the Armor branch.

"Why in the heck are they doing to us what they did to the snake-eaters'" asked one officer familiar with the board's deliberations. "If you ain't Cav, you ain't ought to be wearing a Cav Hat. That just ain't right."

But the sheer functionality of the wide-brimmed American-classic Stetson won over the majority of the board.

"You can keep the sun out of your eyes, the hat won't melt to your head on a sunny day, and female Soldiers can tuck long hair under a Stetson a lot easier than with the current beret," says Stone. "Plus, we've already gone back to blue jackets for the service dress uniform. The Stetson actually completes the look."

The voting of the board fell along predictable lines, but was completed weeks ahead of schedule. In a surprise move representatives from Forts Bragg, Campbell and several undisclosed forward locations around the world pushed the vote for the Stetson to a head...

Stone refused to address rumors that the Army Uniform Board will next consider adoption of a black western-style or "cowboy" boot to replace the current inventory of black low quarters for wear with the Army Service Uniform. Sources expect that if the board moves toward boots, the Armor community will likely push for the return of cavalry-use-only jodhpurs and spurs, as a concession for having lost its prior if informal and exclusive right to wear a Stetson.

There will be some restrictions on wear. In a nod to other dress blue uniform traditions, general officer Stetsons will be black and must have a completely flat brim. All other wearers of dark blue Stetsons will be allowed any combination of opposing but matching curls of the side brims, up-to-twenty-degrees up or down. However, no single-side flapping of any portion of the brim will be allowed.

The Army's official adoption date of the Stetson will be April Fool's Day, 2012.[29]

It is both refreshing and commendable that the United States Army actively embraces a sense of humor.

Photo Accompanying the Army's April Fool's Day Announcement – 2011

---

[29] "Stetson Hat to Be New Army Standard Headgear." 2021. Www.Army.Mil. April 13, 2021.
https://www.army.mil/article/54202/April_Fool_s_2011_story__Stetson_hat_to_be_new_Army_standard_headgear/.

CHAPTER 13
Cav Hat Standards

The Cav Hat is not recognized as official military headwear, and therefore, there are no Army-wide standards or regulations governing its use. The Department of the Army considers the Cav Hat an "Army tradition," as highlighted in a memorandum from the 1st Cavalry Division. Consequently, the commanders of each cavalry unit have the authority to establish their own standards for the appearance and wear of the Cav Hat.

One of the best examples of cavalry hat standards can be found in the 1st Cavalry Division at Fort Hood, Texas. On August 15, 2010, the 1st Cavalry Division issued a memorandum of instruction regarding the proper wearing and appearance of the cavalry hat and spurs. Following is an excerpt from the memorandum's introductory paragraphs:

SUBJECT: Memorandum of Instruction (MOI) Concerning the Wear and Appearance of the CAV Hat and Spurs

1. **PURPOSE:** This MOI defines the general guidelines concerning the wear and appearance of the CAV Hat and Spurs.

2. **APPLICABILITY**: This MOI applies to all Troopers and authorized Civilians in the Division.

3. **BACKGROUND**

> b. The Department of the Army classifies the CAV Hat and Order of the Spur as an "Army tradition." As such, regulations for the awarding of the CAV Hat, Spurs, as well as the wear of Cavalry accoutrements, can be set by a cavalry unit commander. Consequently, lacking any Army-wide regulations, this document provides instructions for all assigned to the 1st Cavalry Division on the proper wear and authorization of such items. Veteran Cavalry Troopers may find that some standards differ slightly from previous units, but the spirit and traditions embodied in this policy memorandum remain the same.

4. **POLICY**

For the most current policy, we shift to the 1st Cavalry Division Standards, "The Yellow Book."

Extracted from the 1st Cavalry Division "Yellow Book," dated May 6, 2025

Wear of the CAV Hat

1. **Who may wear the CAV Hat?** All personnel, military, and DA civilians assigned or attached to the 1CD may purchase and wear the CAV Hat immediately upon arrival to the Division.

2. **Appearance and proper wear of the CAV Hat.**

> a. The CAV Hat can be worn anywhere on-post. It is not authorized for wear off-post except for events designated by a commander.

b. The CAV Hat will be the standard black cavalry hat, Stetson, or other appropriate brand, with a 3-inch brim.

   (1) The hat will present a clean and neat appearance at all times.

   (2) The hat will be formed and shaped so that the front and rear of the brim are either straight or slightly turned down and the sides parallel to the ground and not rounded up "cowboy style." It is recommended that the Trooper go to the 1CD Association Store or the 3CR Gift Shop to have the Stetson shaped properly.

   (3) The crown crease should remain as manufactured. Dimples toward the front of the hat are acceptable so long as they are not creased and present a neat appearance.

c. The black leather neck strap is required for wear. The strap will be worn behind the wearer's head fitting snuggly at the back, lower part of the head. All excess leather will be trimmed and secured.

d. All personnel will wear hat cords according to rank.

   (1) General officers will wear solid gold hat cords.

   (2) Company and field grade officers will wear black and gold hat cords.

   (3) Warrant officers will wear black and silver hat cords; CW5s will wear solid silver hat cords.

   (4) All enlisted Troopers and NCOs will wear either the Cavalry Yellow cord or the color of the cord of their Military Occupational Specialty/Branch of Service.

   (5) Authorized civilians employed by the 1CD will wear cords commensurate with their civil service rating.

(6) Hat cords from the modern era (cords with acorns) are the only authorized cords for Troopers in uniform. The cord will not extend beyond the edge of the brim of the CAV Hat. Cords may be knotted but are not required to distinguish combat service.

e. On the front of the hat, Troopers will wear crossed sabers and rank insignia. These are worn centered on the front of the hat. Rank is worn over the crossed sabers insignia evenly spaced between the top of the hat and the top of the bow ribbon. On the back of the hat, Troopers are only authorized to wear one Distinctive Unit Insignia (DUI), more commonly referred to as unit crest, which will be worn centered on the back of the hat. All active duty and DA civilians assigned to the 1CD will only wear the Unit Crest of the unit they are currently assigned to.

f. Nothing will be worn on the side of the CAV Hat.

g. The CAV Hat will be worn for appropriate occasions. The CAV hat may be worn at all official 1CD functions (e.g., promotions, parades, Stable Calls, or formals, as directed and authorized by the Commanding Officer of the formation). The hat will be the headgear of the day in the 1CD footprint on the last workday of each week, if Troopers choose to purchase it.

(1) The CAV Hat may not be worn during vehicle maintenance.

(2) The CAV Hat may not be worn during field training exercises.

(3) The CAV Hat may be worn during deployments for special events.

(4) The CAV Hat may be worn to, but not inside, a chapel or an area designated for worship during an indoor memorial or religious services. The CAV

Hat may be worn for outdoor services and at these facilities for non-religious events such as 1CD unit functions.

(5) The CAV Hat will be removed when indoors in accordance with U.S. Army headgear regulations unless it is in conjunction with a ceremony, Stable Call, or unit function.

(6) The CAV Hat may be worn in civilian clothing at the wearer's discretion.

(7) The CAV Hat can be worn during parades and ceremonies in lieu of the beret or patrol cap. Unit pride takes precedence over uniformity during formations, parades and ceremonies.[30]

Cav Hat
Image from "The Yellow Book"

---

[30] 1st Cavalry Divisions Standards "The Yellow Book," May 6, 2025, Headquarters, 1st Cavalry Division, Fort Cavavos, Texas (Now Fort Hood).

Rex Gooch

CHAPTER 14
CAV HAT FINALE

The United States Cavalry, now an integral component of the Armor Branch, stands as one of the most dynamic, exhilarating, and innovative combat units of the U.S. Army, embodying a rich legacy of pride and valor. Throughout American history, from the Indian Wars in the late 1800s to contemporary operations in the Middle East, cavalry troops have been instrumental in shaping the outcome of pivotal conflicts, showcasing their unmatched adaptability and strategic significance on the battlefield.

While the cavalry's structure has evolved over the years, its spirit continues to thrive in the mechanized and airmobile forces of the U.S. Army. These legendary units are a powerful testament to the critical importance of mobility, strategy, and leadership in modern warfare. Whether charging on horseback across the plains of the western frontier or flying helicopters over the jungles of Vietnam, the U.S. Cavalry has made a lasting impact on our nation's military history.

Nothing embodies the spirit of the United States Cavalry quite like the cavalry hat. With its rich history and distinguished heritage, the Cav Hat serves as a powerful symbol – a testament to the bravery and enduring traditions of the unit. It represents not just a piece of headwear but a legacy of courage and honor that inspires all who wear it. And those who have earned the privilege of wearing the cavalry hat hold it in the highest regard, considering it one of their most cherished possessions.

While this may conclude the book, the Cav Hat and its enduring legacy lives on. Let us lift a glass to celebrate the United States Cavalry and uphold the enduring legacy of the Cav Hat for generations to come!

APPENDIX I

Vietnam Cav Hat Stories Terminology

Air Cavalry Tactical Colors
Red: Guns
White: Scouts
Blues: Quick reaction force (QRF) inserted by Slicks
Pink Team: One Gunship (red) paired with one Scout helicopter (white)
Heavy Pink Team: Two Guns and two Scouts

Army Aircraft
Loach: OH-6A light observation helicopter (LOH – pronounced "Loach"). This small, nimble helicopter was also called the "Scout." Carried a pilot and one or two gunner/observers.
Cobra: AH-1G attack helicopter, also referred to as "Guns." This heavily armed gunship, crewed by two pilots, carried rockets, miniguns, and/or 40mm grenade launcher.
Huey: UH-1 utility helicopter, the Army's workhorse for troop movement, medevac, and resupply. Referred to as the "Slick" since it carried no heavy armament.

Aviation Terms
AGL: Above ground level, when referring to altitude.
AO: Operations Area or Area of Operation.
Translational Lift: Mode of flight where the helicopter transitions from hovering "ground effect" to forward flight. Additional lift is created by horizontal flow of air across the rotor blades.

Oscar: The observer in a Loach. The oscar is strategically positioned in the front left seat and armed with an M-16 rifle. His role is vigilant reconnaissance and identification of enemy targets.

Torque: The crew chief/door gunner on a Loach. Armed with the M-60 machine gun, the gunner is typically positioned on the right side of the cargo compartment, covering the aircraft during right-hand turns.

QRF: Quick reaction force, a highly specialized, heavily armed team of soldiers deployed by Huey helicopters, rapidly responding to emergencies and developing situations.

Pull Pitch: To pull upward on the collective control in a helicopter, increasing pitch (lift) in the main rotor blades. A term frequently used by pilots meaning to exit promptly.

Mike: An acronym for microphone, also used for miles; i.e., two mikes out and inbound.

Lost his cherry: First time a pilot's aircraft takes hits from enemy fire.

Callsigns

Cavalry troop radio callsigns typically consisted of the troop name followed by a numeral. This numeral indicated the platoon: for instance, scouts were numbered from 11 to 19, Lift from 21 to 29, and Guns from 31 to 39. The troop commander was designated as 6. While this system varied among some troops, the radio callsign clearly identified the individual communicating on the radio.

Corps Areas

The Republic of South Vietnam was divided into four tactical corps areas, from I Corps in the north just below the DMZ to IV Corps in the south, composed of the Mekong Delta.

MACV

Military Assistance Command, Vietnam: Joint-service command of the United States Department of Defense, composed of forces from the United States Army, United States Navy, and United States Air Force, as well as their respective special operations forces.

Other Terms

Arc Light: Codename for Air Force B-52 bombing missions. Missions were commonly flown in three-plane formations known as "cells." Releasing their 750- and 1,000-pound bombs from the stratosphere, the B-52s could neither be seen nor heard from the ground.

DEROS: Date estimated return from overseas.

CAR-15: A short and lightweight variant of the U.S. Army M-16 rifle. Manufactured by Colt, this rifle with retractable buttstock became the iconic weapon of U.S. Army Special Forces in covert operations behind enemy lines. Preferred by pilots due to its smaller size and lighter weight.

Hooch: Slang term for a place to live, either a soldier's living quarters or a Vietnamese hut.

Klicks: Commonly used term for kilometers.

NVA: North Vietnamese Army

O-Club: Officers' club

Strela SA-7: Shoulder-fired, heat-seeking, surface-to-air missile. Introduced by NVA in early 1972, targeting U.S. Army helicopters.

VHPA: Vietnam Helicopter Pilots Association

APPENDIX II

South Vietnam Map

Rex Gooch

INDEX

1st Cavalry Division, 34, 59, 87, 113, 116, 119, 127, 131, 151, 160, 163, 171, 175, 177, 179, 215, 216, 232, 241, 243, 246, 271, 272, 275
Ace Cozzalio, 103
Adolphus McGill, 255
Bill Gillette, 36, 37, 39
Bill Henry, 131, 132
Blackhorse Association, 191, 195
Bob Monette, 69, 71, 90
Bob Smith, 127
Bobby Rinehart, 89
Brave Rifles, 161, 162, 183, 188, 211
Bruce McKenty, 87, 92
Buffalo Soldiers, 23
Bullwhip Squadron, 34, 37, 38, 40
Charles McMenamy, 114
Cliff Lawson, 142
Dick Cross, 45
Don Stivers, 193
Doug Madigan, 81
Frank Walker, 56
Frederic Remington, 185
Garland Hines, 95
Gary Luck, 141
Gary Ryan, 65
General Abrams, 84
Genevieve McCormick, 105
George Abernathy, 113, 117, 253
George Bilafer, 147
Glenn Carr, 95
Greeley Hat Works, 194, 195
Harry Kinnard, 38
Hugh Mills, 135
J.D. Bottorff, 105
James C. Smith, 243
Jim Adamson, 99
Jimmy Ford, 88

Joe Eszes, 97, 100
John B. Stetson Hat Company, 39, 41
John B. Stockton, 34
John Edmunds, 125
John Shafer, 95
John Wayne, 29, 120, 255
John Whitehead, 81
Joseph Pietrzak, 67
Larry Brown, 73
Lighthorse, 103, 105, 156, 157, 205, 206, 207, 208
Lucious Patterson, 107
Major General Glen Walker, 83
Mark Robertson, 66, 67
Michael Goff, 51
Mike Henry, 59, 63
Ned Ricks, 137, 138
Olan Howe, 51, 52
Old Bill, 185
Palehorse, 215, 216, 217
Patrick Laidlaw, 147
Paul Dagnon, 73, 79
Perry Smith, 83, 86
Pete Holmberg, 56
Robert Frank, 119
Robert Hume, 65, 68
Robert Todd Lincoln, 19
Rod Willis, 135
Roger Blaha, 123
Roger Cox, 48
Rough Riders, 25, 26, 27, 231
Russ Miller, 56
Russ Van Houten, 139
Ruthless Riders, 215
Six Shooters, 238, 239
Steve Pullen, 109
Steve Suiter, 123
Terry Tucker, 194
The Fighting Sixth, 221, 222, 223
The Smiling Tigers, 62
Theodore Roosevelt, 25, 27
Walt Harmon, 36
Woodhull Report, 12, 16
Yellow Book, 272, 275

www.ingramcontent.com/pod-product-compliance
Lightning Source LLC
Chambersburg PA
CBHW070634160426
43194CB00009B/1460